Breakthrough Faith

Colin Dye

Hodder & Stoughton
LONDON   SYDNEY   AUCKLAND

10 9 8 7 6 5 4 3

A CIP catalogue record for this title is available
from the British Library.

ISBN 0 340 64250 5

Typeset by Palimpsest Book Production Limited,
Polmont, Stirlingshire
Printed and bound in Great Britain by
Cox & Wyman Ltd, Reading Berkshire

Hodder and Stoughton
A division of Hodder Headline PLC
338 Euston Road
London NW1 3BH

To my wife Amanda, my companion
in faith who lives up to her name:

'worthy to be loved'.

Contents

Acknowledgments

Anyone writing a book on 'Faith' would be bound to make a thousand acknowledgments. Faith comes to us from the Word of God, but it is also shaped by countless people whose contacts with us through the years help make us what we are today. My brother Ray who first showed me the faith in a way I could understand, my 'uncle' Will whose love and gentleness more than anything else won me for Jesus, my mother who insisted on church attendance, my former vicar, the Revd W. Kemp, whose wise words were often missed at the time, but later on in life came back in full force – to all these I owe the beginning of faith, in my life. And since then, I have had my faith strengthened through encouragement and testing by many wonderful people whom the Lord has used more than they can know. Thank you all!

Along with these, I should also like to acknowledge the special help I have had in preparing this manuscript. John Peters, himself a renowned writer, took the time to give firm editorial shape to a series of sermons and the other material specially prepared for the book. Two associates of mine, Chris Cartwright and William Atkinson, payed particular interest in the project. My church, Kensington Temple, is made up of strong men and women of faith, and their prayerful upholding of me at all times, and especially throughout the process of writing, is one of the things I value most of all.

Preface

This book has its source in a series of sermons preached by Colin Dye at Kensington Temple, London, in 1992 and 1993. They had a powerful effect on the congregation there and are now offered to a wider audience in printed form.

Few subjects are as important or as widely written about as faith, but it is a particular pleasure to have a book by someone who combines not only theological awareness with a pastor's heart, but who also moves powerfully in the gifts of the Holy Spirit. Four features of this work are worth mentioning. First, it is *biblically-based*. The Bible is absolutely central to the whole of Colin Dye's ministry, both as preacher and pastor. As he says in chapter 13, the most important lesson of faith is that God's Word is enough. Second, it *applies doctrine to contemporary issues*. Faith, in order to be effective and to become mature, has to be demonstrated in everyday life with all its joys and disappointments. In this sense, Colin Dye sees Abraham as a 'prototype of the life of faith' because the principles of faith are so fully exemplified in his life, responses and attitudes. Third, it is *Christo-centric*. This theological expression means that the Lord Jesus Christ is the heart, the very core, of all the teaching in this book. Its author wants men and women to have a Bible-based faith, to have their lives 'orientated in the way God wants them orientated'. He encourages us to face the right direction, with our feet firmly planted on the *rock of Christ Jesus*. The Gospel that undergirds the book's

perception of faith is comprehensive, proclaiming the
Lord Jesus as *Saviour, Healer, Baptiser in the Holy
Spirit* and *Coming King*. Fourth, it is *balanced*. Colin
Dye does not peddle unrealistic hopes or solutions,
nor does he, on the other hand, minimise the power
of God that's available to every Christian. Nowhere is
this balance more apparent than in the consideration
of the Christian's future hope: the Second Coming of
the Lord Jesus. There is a creative tension between the
'now' of our present existence and the 'not yet' of the
glory that awaits Christians. The 'now' of forgiveness,
healing, physical provision, and the fullness of the Holy
Spirit has to be viewed alongside the constant reminder
and challenge of the 'not yet' of 'the blessed hope'
spoken of in Titus 2:13. Colin Dye says: 'The more
we experience faith in the present, the more our faith
for the future is strengthened, and the more we will
abound in hope by the Holy Spirit'. How appropriate
too is his claim that the way we relate the 'now' and
the 'not yet' is the *key* to successful Christian living.
This is exactly the sort of teaching so urgently needed
in the Christian Church today.

John Peters

Introduction

A breakthrough is 'an act or point of breaking through an obstruction or defensive line; an important advance in knowledge or achievement'.

Today, there are many barriers that faith must overcome. The scepticism and cynicism of our age prevent many Christians from growing sufficiently strong in faith to enjoy the confident assurance before God that Jesus Christ died to make available to us. These enemies of faith attack us at a moment when faith is more needed than ever. The uncertain times in which we live hold us captive and powerless to stand against the 'mega trends' of the world where 'might is right'. As individuals we are lost in a sea of economic, social and moral uncertainty. Rising out of this swirling ocean are the jagged rocks of false religion, self-help psychology and new age practices offered as dangerous modern alternatives to biblical Christianity.

Only faith in Christ will enable us to stand strong in the midst of all that is happening. He has broken the sin barrier and given us a relationship with God. Through Christ we have come to know the truth, finding peace with God and his gift of righteousness that comes to us by faith. But is that all there is to it? Is God only interested in the welfare of our souls? Or is our faith relevant to our lives at every point? This is where many Christians stumble. All are agreed that God is concerned about all our needs, but it seems that we have a long way to go before we experience all that God has made available to us.

Jesus Christ came to bring forgiveness of sins so that we could be in relationship with God as our Heavenly Father who knows about all our needs. He has completely provided for every part of our lives. What else would you expect from this good, kind and loving Father? The provision comes through the promises of God's Word, the Scriptures, and is made available through faith. The whole of the Bible is a call to trust God, not just for our eternal destiny but for our daily provision, for the healing of our bodies, for our security and protection and for our *every* need. All these things go to make up the abundant life Jesus promises his followers. But it is all by faith. Faith is the key.

My prayer is that this book will lead you to the breakthrough you are looking for in your life, in your family and in your own personal situation. It is not a formula for selfish indulgence, for God never blesses that attitude of heart. Rather, it is an attempt to give you some important scriptural keys and spiritual insights which will enable you to advance in your knowledge of God and appreciation of him. God bless you, as you set about achieving great things in your life for him.

Colin Dye
London

1 What is Faith?

*Now faith is the substance of things hoped for,
the evidence of things not seen* (Hebrews 11:1).

Trevor and Sue made their way to the front of the
little church where the pastor was calling people to
accept Christ. Like many people today, they had a
little knowledge of Christian things but no idea that it
was possible to have a personal relationship with Jesus
Christ. They had been contacted and brought to the
service through the widening network of enthusiastic
young people eager to tell their friends about Jesus.
Some of these friends gathered around Trevor and
Sue as they prayed a simple prayer confessing their
new-found faith in Christ.

After this, they looked up beaming with joy. Sue's
dark brown eyes filled up as Trevor put his arm around
her shoulder. They knew something very beautiful had
just happened. The pastor continued, 'You have begun
a journey, an adventure of faith. God has called you to
live from now on each day not for yourselves but for
the Lord who has saved you. Faith is not just praying
a prayer to accept Christ in your life, it is submitting
to his Lordship, letting him have complete control.'

These words did not come as a surprise. Trevor and
Sue had thought long and hard about their decision to
become Christians. They knew the implications were
to be far-reaching and life-changing. They had indeed
begun a journey, but they were not alone. They had

received the Holy Spirit as their divine companion and the small church fellowship was on hand to offer constant help and encouragement. The pastor visited them often giving them carefully prepared Bible study material and answering the many questions that growing Christians ask.

Every day thousands enter this same journey of faith from all walks of life and from all over the world. It is a journey that is as old as the Bible itself, going back to Abraham's time and beyond. And yet, as Trevor and Sue found, it is up to date and relevant today. Four thousand years ago God spoke to Abraham, saying, 'Get out of your country . . . and come to a land that I will show you' (Acts 7:3). That was the beginning of his adventure of faith. He did not know what lay ahead, but he had the certainty that in the midst of everything, God was with him, and 'by faith Abraham obeyed when he was called . . . and went out, not knowing where he was going' (Hebrews 11:8).

In the same way Trevor and Sue, both in their early 20s, could never have known what lay ahead for them. They had turned the direction of their life towards Christ and had received forgiveness of sins. But did faith mean more than that? What about the practical details of their lives? They were unemployed and had been fairly satisfied to live off state benefit payments. Now they were not sure. Sue had suffered repeated episodes of illness, including glandular fever, which left her weak and at times very depressed. Could God help her at this level, or was Christianity only about 'spiritual' issues?

Whether young or mature in the Christian faith, we all ask these same questions. The Bible is a practical handbook for life, but does it offer real solutions to the real needs of our lives? Is faith just a ticket to heaven, or does it also offer hope for our life on earth? These are crucial questions which must be answered if we are going to have a meaningful faith for today. We need to know where to turn in times of uncertainty in the midst of the shifting sands of human values and belief systems. Faith is extremely precious in this unbelieving world and we need to hold on to it against its many assailants. Above all faith must be real if it is going to flourish in the modern environment so hostile to it. But to be real it must also be part of our daily experience. Faith must show us how to live under the day-by-day pressures and have something to say to us in every circumstance of life.

Faith is about giving to God what pleases him. Letting God hear our earthly affirmations of his heavenly truth, giving to him our confidence despite the threats of unemployment and illness, despite problems in our marriage and family or the financial difficulties we may be facing. It is also being willing to believe God in the midst of an uncertain world. And God for his part offers us the rewards of faith, his provision for our every need. The source of this kind of faith is not human effort or activity. The New Testament shows that although faith is the responsibility of men and women (Hebrews 3:18–19), it comes from Jesus, the author of our faith (Hebrews 12:2), as the gift of God (Ephesians 2:8–9), and as the work of the Holy Spirit (2 Corinthians 1:20).

It is important to mention these basic principles at the start of this book. Many people think that faith is about trying hard to get something from God; it isn't. It involves the whole of our lives lived in simple dependence on God, in a way that pleases him. At the heart of that is an attitude of faith, for without fait/h it is impossible to please God (Hebrews 11:6).

The opposite of faith is to dis-believe God. Jesus addressed this issue when his disciples seemed, through their unbelief, incapable of healing a young boy who had a deaf and dumb spirit. They asked Jesus why they could not cast it out and he told them it was because they had little faith. But he also addressed the crowd that assembled there and said, 'Don't criticise my disciples. They are after all learning faith. But you are an unbelieving and perverse generation' (see Luke 9:41).

When I read that one day, I said to myself, 'That's a bit strong!' But the Holy Spirit showed me that when we fail to believe God, we are imputing unrighteousness to him. Now that's perverse – to call the One who is altogether righteous, totally unfaithful to his Word, the God who can never lie, the God who has all power and authority – to call him a liar and to disbelieve his Word must be a perverted thing indeed. Yet the truth is that all Christians struggle at times with this whole area of belief. We need the Lord to lead us from unbelief to faith and to help us grow through the various stages of faith to attain the goal.

Levels of faith

The Bible speaks about little faith, great faith, and there is such a thing as mature or perfect faith. Jesus said to his disciples on many occasions, 'O you of little faith. Where is your faith?' (Luke 8:24–5). He marvelled at their unbelief. In Nazareth he was unable to do any mighty work there because of their unbelief. Britain, like Nazareth, is an environment of unbelief. How different I feel when I visit places like Africa, where my faith rises the minute I step off the plane. I look for the nearest sick person. Sometimes in Africa it is exceptional for people *not* to be healed, whereas in Britain and much of the rest of Europe, our self-righteousness sees fit to reject what these people are hungry for. Western Christians are so sophisticated, and God wants to deal with that. He wants us to humble ourselves and ask him for a new anointing of faith.

Little faith is weak and faltering, whereas great faith is strong and gets things done. Jesus found great faith present in the centurion who asked him to heal his servant. This man was not a Jewish believer, and we have no indication that he even had any knowledge of the God of Israel, but he recognised that Jesus had authority. So he said, 'Don't come into my house. I'm not worthy of such a thing. Just speak the word and my servant will be healed. I know that it will happen because I'm under authority myself and I'm a man over people. When I say "Go!" they go.' Jesus said, 'I've not seen faith as great as this in all Israel', and of course he healed the servant (Matthew 8:10). Christians need to offer God faith like that today. I am convinced that God is sending an anointing of faith upon his Church in these last days so we will be able to perform the mighty works of God in our generation. Then we will see the body of Christ rise up as a powerful force in society.

In chapter two, we will look in more detail at the different levels of faith, but first we need to be clear about the meaning of the word 'faith'.

What is faith?

Hebrews 11:1 says that faith is 'the substance of things hoped for, the evidence of things not seen'. According to this verse, faith is occupied with the 'not yet' and with 'the unseen'. This is precisely where most of us go wrong. The world's philosophy says that seeing is believing, but the Bible says believing is seeing. If we can see it, we don't need to believe God for it. We have it already. The writer of Hebrews tells us that faith is the substance of things *hoped for*.

Faith and hope

The Bible uses the word 'hope' to describe a confident expectation of a future event and the certainty of that future condition. An obvious example is the resurrection of the body. It has not yet happened, but it is going to happen. We know that because when Jesus was raised from the dead he released the hope of resurrection, which means one day we will all be raised from the dead. It's our glorious hope, and is linked to the future return of Jesus Christ (see Titus 2:13).

The Apostle Paul speaks about hope in Romans 8:24: 'For we were saved in this hope.' We are not just saved by faith. We are saved by (or in) hope, because we've not yet received everything that will be ours through the salvation in Jesus Christ. But as Paul says, 'Hope that is seen is not hope; who hopes for what he already has?' In other words, as long as it is future, as long as it's not yet come to pass, we can call it 'hope'.

Hebrews 11:1 specifies faith is *the evidence of things not seen*. Faith's province is the 'not yet' and the 'unseen'. That's why we struggle with it. The Bible says we are called to live by faith, not by sight. Most people when they pray concentrate only on the immediate physical results, rather than focusing on what God says. Unless we know how to believe when the thing is invisible, we will never see it happen. First we believe, then we receive.

There's an excellent illustration of this principle in the Old Testament, which Paul highlights in Romans 4:13–21. Abraham faced the fact that his body was as good as dead and that Sarah was barren and childless. Nevertheless he was strong in faith regarding the promise of God, being fully persuaded that what God had promised, he was able to do. He faced the facts, but in the knowledge that they were not the whole truth of the situation. Here Abraham realises that *spiritual truth goes far beyond physical facts.* God had named him Abraham, father of a multitude, and he clung onto the truth of that as the days passed and nothing appeared to be happening. He had faith in the God who calls things that are not, as though they already were. He said, 'I have faith in a God who will not allow any of his promises to fail. God will yet perform in my body what I have received in my heart by faith.' And in due time, Sarah conceived.

This condition, of knowing that we have received something from God in advance of the manifestation of it, is just like being pregnant. We carry the promise in our hearts as an unseen, yet accomplished reality. We can't see it, or feel it, but we know by faith it is ours. This principle is part of our daily Christian walk. We can't see Jesus but he is with us always. We know him personally and intimately by faith. We talk to him and hear from him. That's the essence of faith; it has to do with the invisible realm.

Faith is substantial

Many people think that faith is make-believe, like the schoolboy who was asked by the teacher, 'What is faith?' Thinking for a moment about the school chapel where the assembly had just recited the Apostles' Creed, he replied, 'Sir, it's believing something you know isn't true!' No. Faith does not have the status of a fairy story. Neither is it wishful thinking – convincing ourselves that something is true as if that were going to make it become true. That's not faith at all, but mere positive thinking. Faith is *substance*, because it is based on what has to come to us by revelation. Substance, whatever else it is, is something we can get hold of. Faith is solid and is substantial.

The substance of faith

The word for substance carries at least three strands of meaning. The first is borrowed from Greek philosophy where substance means 'things as they really are, not as they appear to be'. If we only look at things as they appear to be, we will never move in faith.

Another meaning of the word is 'a firm foundation'. Because faith is substantial we can walk, stand and build our lives on it. That's what happened to Peter when he walked on the water. Actually, he walked on faith in the Word of Jesus. Because the Lord had instructed Peter to come, he was able to exercise faith in the Word of God and that foundation of faith was so strong it enabled him to walk on water. By faith we can do the impossible because by it we experience the power of God. Everything else will let us down, but real faith will never let us down. It's an unshakeable foundation for our lives.

Another use of substance is taken from the world of commerce and property. The word was used for the title deed of a piece of land or building. If we have the title deed to our property it is proof that we own the house. It doesn't prove that we actually live in the house; somebody else could live there. We may not be the occupier but we are the *owner*. So when we are exercising faith we lay hold of the title deed to our promise and, by faith, make the transition from being the owner to the occupier. In other words we lay claim to our property and take possession of it.

Sometimes our 'faith-property' is taken over by squatters, or illegal tenants who have to be evicted! Then we take the title deed relating to the promise and say to the enemy, 'Get out of my house, I'm coming to occupy that which is mine.' If he resists, we simply take him to court and we execute God's written judgment concerning him (Psalm 149:9). We say, 'Father God, your Word declares this is my property. I want you to give me judgment in this. It's my house, my name is on the title deed, you have given it to me. I am the owner, but the occupier refuses to go.' And the Lord says, '*You* go back there in the authority of my name and *you* tell him from me, he's got to go!'

We must get hold of the title deed to the promises God has made over our lives, our loved ones, over our cities and over our nations. God has given the promises to us, the title deeds are ours. Through faith the things hoped for become an experienced reality. God's promises are fulfilled by faith. Faith doesn't make them true but faith enables us to take and enjoy them.

Faith is evidence

Finally, faith is *evidence*. Evidence is used to prove a case, and the word used for evidence here means 'strong evidence or proof', so that beyond any doubt whatsoever the person under trial is proved guilty. It refers to incontrovertible evidence, evidence that cannot be denied. A related word is conviction. The evidence is so solid that it has been made to stick and brings about a conviction. In the same way, faith is the evidence of things not seen. Many people in our society are saying if the Bible is true, prove it; but I tell you, faith *is* the evidence.

When I was a Bible college student, I would frequently witness on the streets of Cambridge. Some-times, intellectual people came to challenge what I was saying. One man stood near to me and said, 'I'm an atheist, I'm a communist and I'm a scientist!' He went through every philosophy in the book so long as it was anti-God. And then he said, 'I won't believe without proof!' I replied, 'Oh, you want proof? I've got proof.' He laughed cynically, but I turned him to the passage in Hebrews and read, 'Faith is the substance of things hoped for, the evidence of things not seen.' He was looking for physical proof as if he could put God in a test tube. But our God is bigger than his test tube!

Faith then, is truth. It is reality. It is evidence, not make-believe. We need to enter into the full conviction of faith and put away the half-hearted kind of faith that permeates much of the Christian Church today. Let's begin by believing our nation belongs to Jesus Christ and that we can take it for him. He has commanded us to do so, and has paid for it by the blood of his cross. I would like to share a faith-conviction that we are seeking to see fulfilled in our city, London. In our church we often declare, 'London belongs to the Lord Jesus Christ and not the devil!' We then follow through this declaration seriously, by reaching out to those who are lost and hurting without Christ.

We work with the unemployed, people with AIDS and the homeless, as well as those with a degree of worldly security. We are planting out new groups and local fellowships at the rate of more than one each week. And all because we believe that God has given us this city to save and to serve. This robust approach to faith has been taught us by many in the so-called developing world, who actually dare to believe God and act on their belief. In Nigerian Lagos, Kenyan Nairobi and the Brazilian city Sao Paulo, I have seen whole cities being impacted through the simple but potent faith of ordinary believers, reaching out in confidence to others. We must begin to occupy that which by faith we possess, and expect it to happen! We may not be ready to start with a whole city, but we *can* start with ourselves, our life, our family, our street.

Moving on in Hebrews 11:1, we come to the next phrase, 'the evidence of *things not seen*'. Here is where I really praise God for my study of the Greek text of the New Testament, because reading in the original one day I came across this phrase that is often missed. In English it reads, 'faith is the substance of *things* hoped for – just '*things*'. But the Bible doesn't just say *things*. The word that lies behind that translation is a powerful one. It means 'accomplished facts, truths or realities'. Therefore, faith is the substance of God's accomplished truths and his invisible realities.

Accomplished realities

Everything that we need for life and godliness, from forgiveness of sins to every other earthly provision, has been promised by the Father in the Word and purchased by Christ on the cross. When we understand this and see that every promise of the Bible is actually an accomplished truth before him, then by faith we can reach into the invisible realm and lay hold of God's spiritual realities concerning our life. By faith we take them and bring them into the realm of the actual, visible world of our own human experience.

When Jesus died on the cross he declared 'It is finished!' (John 19:30), which means it is accomplished, the debt has been paid. On the cross he purchased our full salvation which begins with forgiveness of sins. The moment we reach out by the hand of faith into the invisible realm and lay hold of God's accomplished truth concerning our forgiveness, we are forgiven. This is what Trevor and Sue received that night at the front of the church. But God's salvation doesn't stop there. There are other promises and other blessings that follow.

Once Trevor and Sue had resolved to follow a life of faith, they began to understand and receive some of the other provisions of God for their lives. They discovered that every blessing that God has for us on the earth has already been accomplished on the cross of Jesus Christ. Sue began to lay claim to physical healing believing that Jesus paid for it on the cross. Her health dramatically improved. Trevor began to pray about his job situation knowing that God had promised to provide for all their needs. He started voluntary work, improving some previously-acquired skills in graphic design. He persevered until he eventually received some pay for his work and then went into business for himself. He struggled at first to make ends meet, but felt the encouragement of the Lord all the way. Now, fifteen years after their original commitment to Christ, Trevor's business is prospering and he is serving as an elder in his local church. Sue has a ministry among young people in the fellowship and has no recurring health problem.

The Lord honoured their faith and persistence. They laid hold of *God's* accomplished truth, not their own imagination or wishes for their lives. Faith is not trusting our mental power or our desires, but is responding to God's Word. Every promise in the Bible that God has spoken in our life is our rightful possession and he has accomplished it in the cross of Jesus Christ. So the things that are truly hoped for are not just what we might like to invent for ourselves: 'That's a good idea, I think I'll have it.' Don't think anything unless it is God's thought. That's the difference between truth and fantasy, faith and presumption.

Once we understand this basic principle we are set to experience real breakthrough in our lives. We go beyond the mentality that plays down the significance of our physical needs and remember that Jesus is Lord over all of life. He has his solutions to our practical as well as our spiritual problems. Once we see what by faith is available to us we will never settle for anything less than God's best for every area of our lives. We will want to go on to possess all the spiritual truths and practical realities which God has given to us. That's breakthrough faith.

2 Breakthrough Faith

So Jesus answered and said to them, 'Have faith in God' (Mark 11:22).

The kind of breakthroughs that Trevor and Sue experienced did not come easy. They had to grow in their faith and understanding, and learn to stand firm during many tests, but God came through for them every time. Soon after Trevor began to receive a regular income, Sue spoke of her secret dream, to buy a house and settle down in the beautiful town on the south coast of England where they lived. 'We can't afford it,' protested Trevor, but Sue was unperturbed. They agreed to pray about it and put aside what little they could towards a possible deposit.

It was a couple of years before they had enough for a down payment on the smallest of the properties on the market at the time. Led by Sue's enthusiasm, they went house hunting. One property stood out among the rest. It was everything that Sue hoped for. 'Trevor, that's the house for us, I'm sure!' she said excitedly. Trevor was more careful, 'I'm not so sure. It's way out of our reach,' replied Trevor cautiously. 'Come on, Trevor. Where's your faith!' was Sue's determined answer. So they agreed to pray about it. After a while they both felt the quiet confidence of the Holy Spirit that somehow God was going to make it possible for them to have that house. In faith, they went ahead, believing the Lord to make up the several thousand pounds shortfall.

Tension began to mount over the next few weeks as the deadline drew closer and closer. But no money came. Finally, the agent told them the bad news. Unless they could come up with the full funds by noon on Friday, in two days' time, they would lose the house. It seemed totally impossible, but their faith held out. 'It will be there!' they told themselves. Friday came and Trevor went to work as usual wondering what the day would bring. Around eleven in the morning, Sue was on the phone, beside herself with excitement. 'Trevor, you'll never guess what. The money has come!' She went on to explain that someone had come round for coffee less than two hours before the deadline and had left a gift. It was exactly the sum of money needed to complete the deal on the house. God had answered their prayers. The donor had no idea about their financial need. It was God who honoured Trevor and Sue's faith.

No wonder Jesus said, 'Have faith in God.' Such a God inspires our confidence and deserves us to honour him with strong faith. Faith cannot be manufactured, it 'comes by hearing and hearing by the word of God' (Romans 10:17). But it is our responsibility to grow in faith so that we move from weak faith to stronger faith. We must get rid of all our unbelief. To achieve this the emphasis must be more on the God of faith than on faith itself. God is the one who develops our faith. Before Trevor and Sue had accepted Christ, they had been affected by the secular values of the day. In their own way they were both quite cynical. But their unbelief was swept away by the truth of God's Word making room for God to work. What had begun as a mustard seed was now becoming a strong tree capable of carrying many things.

In order to experience breakthrough faith, we must be prepared to deal with the obstructions of unbelief and weak faith. We must allow God to grow faith in us as we hold on to his Word every step of the way. Throughout their time with Jesus in the gospels, the disciples struggle against unbelief. Personally, I fight this every day of my life, as I see the tendency within me to reject the Word of God. My human nature sets itself against the truth of God and plays host to doubt and unbelief. God wants to help us overcome this and grow in faith. My constant prayer is 'Lord, I believe; help my unbelief!' (Mark 9:24).

Unbelief

Any unbelief on our part is an attack on God's integrity. The Bible declares that God is absolutely true. He is light and in him is no darkness at all. He is a God who cannot change, who doesn't lie, and who is totally faithful in fulfilling his promises. The omnipotent, all-powerful God of the universe, backs up his Word by his power, and so any response on our part which minimises God or doubts his Word is very serious. As Numbers 23:19 says, 'God is not a man, that He should lie, nor a son of man, that He should repent. Has He said, and will He not do? Or has He spoken, and will He not make it good?'

We are far too casual about unbelief in the Western world giving too much place to scepticism and even prizing intellectual doubt. I often joke with my congregation and say British Christians are full of roast beef and unbelief! Rather than entertaining such thoughts we should be taking the Word of God at face value and living by the truth of the Scriptures.

In the gospels, Jesus constantly encourages people to grow into greater levels of faith. In Mark chapter 6, Jesus visits his own home town of Nazareth where he is greeted by a wave of apathy. Put off by the fact that they remember him in his youth, they say scornfully, 'Isn't this Mary's child, we know him, his brothers and sisters are here', and so they stumbled because of this familiarity. What was working behind this was lack of faith. It actually says in Mark 6:5: 'Now He could do no mighty work there, except that He laid His hands on a few sick people and healed them.' There is a connection between their lack of faith and their inability to receive from God. That inability to receive from God also limited what Christ himself was able to do for them.

On one occasion a man brought his demon-afflicted son to Jesus and said, 'Your disciples couldn't cast the demon out. If there is anything *you* can do, please help me.' Jesus looked out across the crowd that had gathered and said, 'Oh faithless and perverse generation, how long shall I be with you and bear with you?' (Luke 9:41). Is there anything more perverse than human beings who are created in the image of the God, whose every breath comes as his gracious gift and who receive his daily provisions of goodness, then refuse him when he speaks to them? Man is so weak, so puny, so finite by comparison to the eternal, uncreated God, and yet we would listen to God's Words and say, 'I don't believe it.' Jesus identifies it accurately, 'You *perverse* generation.'

Unbelief is rooted in our sinful human nature. We entertain a stubborn refusal to believe. Throughout his ministry, Jesus told his disciples that he was going to die and be raised again from the dead, but when it happened they did not believe it. Jesus had told his disciples to meet him in Galilee after he had been raised from the dead. But they didn't do it; instead, they remained in Jerusalem. The women who had gone to the tomb went to the disciples and reported that they had seen Jesus, but they still didn't believe. Other reports came flooding in to the disciples, including the account of the two who had met Jesus on the road to Emmaus. They went back and told the rest but they were not believed either. Afterwards, Jesus himself appeared to the eleven as they sat at the table while they were eating and he rebuked them for their lack of faith and their *stubborn refusal to believe*. At the very heart of our rebellious human nature lies this same stubborn refusal to believe. We cannot believe God with our natural faculties alone, it takes a supernatural work of the Holy Spirit.

Weak faith

Another level of faith is weak or faltering faith. This description may be applied to many Christians today. One minute they are up, the next they are down. When things are going well they are praising God and full of faith until, that is, they encounter the slightest opposition or difficulty. When facing ridicule at work or some personal obstacle, they cave in. They are doing fine until some newspaper discredits a prominent evangelist, or some new liberal view of who they suppose Jesus really is gets published in a popular magazine and suddenly faith is shaken. This is so sad because our faith is not founded on intellectual trends but on the Word of God, which lives and abides for ever (Isaiah 40:8).

Jesus addresses the issue of weak faith in the Sermon on the Mount when he asks why we run around, anxiously trying to gain the things that God is willing to provide for us anyway. He points to the birds of the air and the flowers of the field and reminds us that our heavenly Father feeds the birds of

the air and clothes the flowers of the field. Not even
Solomon in all his glorious splendour was clothed like
they are. And so, Jesus says in Matthew 6:30: 'Now
if God so clothes the grass of the field, which today
is, and tomorrow is thrown into the oven, will He not
much more clothe you? O, you of little faith.' Weak
faith leads us to worry excessively about the ordinary
circumstances of life. What are we going to eat? Where
are we going to live? What are we going to wear? What
about tomorrow? Instead of this, God is calling us to
believe him in a strong way, expecting him to fulfil his
Word to us and all the time growing in faith. Strong
faith is built by focusing on God and his kingdom,
while trusting his provision for our temporal needs.
As Jesus says, 'Seek first the kingdom of God and
His righteousness, and all these things will be added
to you.'

It is so often fear that holds our faith back, keeping
it from developing. The New Testament exposes fear
as an enemy of faith. Take, as an example, Matthew
8 where Jesus is in the boat. It is a fascinating story
because the storm rages in the middle of the lake and
the disciples begin to panic. All the while, Jesus is
asleep in the back of the boat but finally, they wake
him: 'Lord, save us! We are going to die!' Jesus' reply
is recorded in verse 26: 'Why are you so fearful, O
you of little faith?' Then he got up and rebuked the
winds and the waves and it was completely calm. Of
course, they should have known that if Jesus was there
he was going to look after them and he wasn't going
to let anything happen.

In Luke's gospel, we read that they had more than
the presence of Jesus in the boat, they also had his
Word, 'Let us cross over to the other side of the lake'
(Luke 8:22). This is exactly the same for us today; we
have his Word and his Spirit with us. Why be afraid?

Fear drives out faith. On the other hand, if we take faith and grow in it, then fear is driven out. Fear and faith are opposites: 'Do not be afraid, only believe!' (Mark 5:36).

Great faith

The opposite of weak faith is great faith. Great faith may be defined as recognising who Jesus really is: he is the Lord of the universe; he is the great King, the God of the nations, whose authority is unquestionable.

Do you remember the story in Matthew 8 about the centurion who comes to Jesus and says, 'My servant is sick.'? Jesus replies, 'Let me come with you and I will heal him.' But the centurion refuses, 'No, I don't need you to do that. I am not worthy for you to come into my house. You are a man of authority, as I am a man of authority. I have people under me and I have people over me and if I say to my servant, this is what you are to do the servant obeys. All you need to do is to speak the word and it shall be done.' When Jesus heard this, he was astonished, and told those following him, 'I have not found such great faith, not even in Israel!'

What a tragedy. The very people that should have been moving in strong faith actually were full of unbelief. I can remember many situations when I have found it much easier to minister to people whom we would not expect to have faith. Non-Christians are sometimes more prepared to take us at our word than Christians who are supposed to have faith. If we say 'God heals the sick', many unbelievers say 'OK, pray for me then.' But the believers will give us twenty-seven reasons why it's not going to work! There seem to be so many negative influences to block our faith, and God wants to break them down and release us to develop strong faith that overcomes.

The other great example in the gospels of this level of faith came from a woman who was also not from Israel. A Gentile woman from Canaan came to Jesus and cried out, 'Have mercy on me, O Lord, Son of David! My daughter is severely demon-possessed' (Matthew 15:22). Finally the exasperated disciples came to Jesus and said, 'Get rid of her, Lord, she is bothering us!' Jesus answered her, 'I was not sent, except for the lost sheep of the house of Israel.' But she became all the more insistent and fell down before him saying, 'Lord help me!' But he answered again with the words, 'It is not good to take the children's bread and throw it to the little dogs.' Then she replied, 'Yes, that's true, but even the dogs eat from the crumbs which fall under the master's table!'

The average church member today would have been offended by such treatment at the hand of a so-called man of God and would have gone off in a huff to find another church. But not this woman. The Lord often 'offends the mind to reveal the heart' and having seen what was inside this woman, he was amazed at her faith: 'O Woman, great is your faith! Let it be to you as you desire', and her daughter was healed at that very hour. The greatness of this woman's faith was that she would not be put off; she was persistent. She refused to be discouraged and held on to the principle that God was willing to bless. She was not going to take 'No' for an answer. This is the essence of great faith.

Unbelieving West?

What has choked the life out of our faith as Western Christians? Is it the fact that we have everything we need without trusting God? Most Christians seem anxious only to ensure they have their ticket to heaven, and everything else they need is provided by today's affluent society. In contrast, many people in Africa, India, Asia and parts of South America are more obviously dependent on God. The humble poor believe, while the rich and arrogant put their trust in their personal wealth, status and superior education. What an indictment on us! All our Western values, education and scientific knowledge have produced is arrogant self-assertion against God who made us and gives us the very breath we breathe. Centrally, the issue is one of pride and self-reliance. The centurion, for all his authority and status, was ready to accept the superior authority of Jesus. He not only recognised Jesus' authority, but he also submitted himself to it by asking the Lord to exercise it on his behalf.

Perfect faith

As we go through the New Testament we find that there is yet a further level of faith: perfect or mature faith. This is the kind of faith that moves mountains, overcomes obstacles, is triumphant through trials and holds on, not weakened by circumstances, but presses through for as long as is necessary to receive the answer from God. It is breakthrough faith. In Mark chapter 11 Jesus speaks of this kind of faith when he says, 'Have faith in God.' Here at once we see perfect faith at work. It has the power to move mountains and yet, as a similar passage from the gospel shows, it is only mustard seed faith. The emphasis is on *quality faith*, not on how much faith we can muster up ourselves. The focus is on God and not on man.

Never have faith in faith but have faith in God. He has the power, the capacity and the solutions. Some translate the phrase as, 'Have the faith of God', meaning 'Have the God-kind of faith, the faith that God gives.' This kind of faith is Holy Spirit inspired and is perfect, powerful and pure, because it welcomes God into the situation. It is not mixed with doubt or supposition. It clings to the revealed will of God and shuns all presumption, but once it is fixed like a missile homing device, it always finds its target. Such is faith's clarity; such is faith's certainty. We need this capacity to see clearly in today's world.

We live in a society where there are no certainties – only shifting values and changing ideas. In contrast, mature faith lays hold of God's certainties in the midst of all of this and stands tall on a secure foundation, confident that God will fulfil his Word. The Word of God carries within it the power of its own fulfilment. All we have to do is to open our hearts, receive his Word in childlike simplicity and God does the rest. He begins to grow our faith and challenge it through tests and trials. These come to develop its strength and integrity. The more intense the trials, the more triumphant the faith. We see God dealing this way with all the great men and women of faith, until faith emerges tried and tested, strong and mature.

And all this brings him glory. Faith is not an end in itself, or even ultimately for our own benefit, but for God. By faith we can achieve great things for God and his kingdom on earth.

3 What Faith Does

All things are possible to him who believes
(Mark 9:23).

Norman Warren was the new curate at St Paul's
Church, Leamington Spa, situated in the British midlands. He had an intense desire to see ordinary people
come to faith in Christ, and yet he knew that there
were many obstacles in the way. The Church in Britain
had a reputation for being remote and irrelevant. As
Norman began to pray about his burden for the lost,
he felt overpowered by the enormity of the task, but
God gave him courage. And then the idea came: he
would write a short booklet, explaining the Gospel
in a straightforward and understandable way. He set
about writing and soon the booklet, *Journey into Life*
was born. Norman distributed it in the local parish and
found it was an effective tool in spreading the good
news. Soon other parishes took it up and the booklet
gained wider and wider circulation.

Today, thirty years later over ten million copies of
Norman's booklet have been distributed. It has been
translated into more than sixty languages and has
helped many thousands of people come to faith in
Christ. When he first wrote Norman could never have
known how God was going to use it. But God rewarded
this simple act of faith with astounding results.

God is the God of the impossible. He inspires faith
within us enabling us to recognise that he is who he

says he is and will do what he says he will do, no matter how impossible it is by human standards. When we believe, we are simply acknowledging that what God says is true. Real faith is laying hold of God's power. It is not a matter of mind control, or mind over matter, or positive thinking. Rather, through having a personal relationship with Jesus Christ, we enjoy God's faith operating in our lives. And because it is God's faith, it achieves great results.

Faith pleases God

In Hebrews 11:6 it says, 'Without faith, it is impossible to please God.' That means without faith it is impossible to experience God, live the Christian life, or to honour him. With faith, however, all things become possible. Suddenly the promises of God that seemed so remote and out of reach become real and actual in our daily experience. We must never underestimate the place that faith has. I am not suggesting that faith itself achieves these things; it is not faith in *faith*, but faith in *God*.

All things are possible

Jesus makes some astonishing statements about faith. He says to a woman healed of a long-standing illness, 'Your faith has made you well' (Matthew 9:21–2). He says to two blind men, 'According to your faith, let it be to you' (Matthew 9:29). He also says, 'And all things, whatever you ask in prayer, believing, you will receive' (Matthew 21:22). He spoke to another man and said, 'All things are possible to him who believes' (Mark 9:23). Jesus said to a man healed of leprosy, 'Arise, go your way. Your faith has made you well' (Luke 17:19). He spoke to someone else and said, 'Did I not say to you that if you would believe you would see the glory of God?' (John 11:40). He also said, 'He who believes in me, the works that I do he will do also; and greater works than these he will do, because I go to My Father' (John 14:12). Also, in the days of the early church, as Peter made it clear, miracles like the lame man healed at the temple, came by faith in the name of Jesus (Acts 3:16).

Throughout the whole of the New Testament, faith is shown to be of paramount importance, and we need to grasp this message with fresh clarity and conviction today. We mustn't overemphasise faith, by making it an end in itself; but we must have faith if we want to begin to do significant things for the glory of God and his kingdom. We must have the living faith seen in the gospels so that the impossible might happen today. Four examples from the gospels will help to emphasise this truth.

Internal bleeding

Matthew chapter 9 records the story of the woman who had suffered with a bleeding problem for twelve years. She had gone to all kinds of doctors, and nobody had been able to help her. The problem was beyond human hope. She knew that there was nothing more she could do – she had done everything possible, spending all her money on doctors. Nothing had worked, and she was getting worse.

Then she heard about Jesus, and so she said, 'I am going to go to him to get help from him.' But according to Jewish customs, there was a great obstacle in her way. Because she was ceremonially unclean it would have been totally wrong for her to allow Jesus to touch her, and what is more, the crowd around Jesus prevented it. Suddenly, she said to herself, 'If I could just touch the hem of his garment, I will be made completely whole.' So, fixed with that one thought of getting close to Jesus in her mind, she began to push through the crowds. Now she must have been completely exhausted and in a state of extreme physical weakness, but her faith enabled her to be persistent until at last she broke through the crowds. When she finally touched Jesus' clothes something happened! The Lord turned around abruptly, and asked, 'Who touched me?' The disciples answered, 'What are you talking about, everybody is touching you', but he said, 'No. *Someone* touched me.'

Many people that day were touching Jesus, probably every one of them with a need for healing or for something else in their lives, and yet *it was the touch of faith* that made the difference. We need to understand that without faith we are not going to be blessed, we are not going to receive from God. Without faith the promises of God are not going to be active in our lives. Faith activates the promises of God and this woman was healed as a result of it. Look at the words of Jesus himself: 'Take heart, daughter, *your faith* has healed you.' And the woman was healed from that moment.

Now that is a statement that many Christians today would be afraid to make, because they know faith has no power in itself to heal or give the blessing. This woman was healed by the power of Christ, not the power of faith; but her faith was the means of reaching out to God and experiencing his power. Without that vital connection the woman would have remained unhealed. The cable connection brings the power to your television set which cannot operate without it, but the cable is not the *source* of the power. In the same way faith connects us to the power of God, and his promises do not operate in our lives without it.

Seeing

Again, in Matthew 9, two blind men came to Jesus for healing and he asked them, 'Do you believe I am able to do this?' Jesus always looks for faith in those he blesses. He knows that without faith, we are not going to receive. Faith is the empty hand that receives; the attitude that accepts 'I cannot do this myself, I need you, Lord.' The blind men opened their hearts in belief and said, 'Yes, Lord, we do believe you are going to heal us.' Then he touched their eyes and said, 'According to your faith will it be done to you.' And they were healed at that very moment!

Walking

Four men brought their paralysed friend to Jesus in faith, and he acted. 'Son, your sins are forgiven you', he said (Mark 2:5), and then he healed him. When they carried this man to Jesus, it was their faith that was operating. They thought, 'This man is going to be healed.' Mark records that it was 'when Jesus *saw their faith*' that he acted. Real faith is visible, expressed in actions, and that kind of faith gets answers! In the same way, when we pray, our faith can carry people to Jesus.

Hearing

Mark 9 contains the story of the man who brought his son who had a deaf and dumb spirit to Jesus to be healed. Jesus was absent and his disciples were unable to help them. Then when Jesus returned, the man said, 'Your disciples are unable to heal my boy. If you can do anything, would you do it?' Jesus replied, 'If you can? Everything is possible for him who believes' (Mark 9:23 NIV). Here Jesus was saying, 'It is not a question of whether I am capable of doing this or not. Of course I can do it. All things are possible, but only if *you* believe.' That is the condition for releasing God's power in our life.

Many Christians today are sitting back waiting for God to act, with an almost fatalistic attitude: 'If God wants to do it, he will do it.' Hiding behind false theology they say, 'We can't be sure of God's will.' But all the time God is saying, 'I *am* able and I *am* willing. But are *you* willing to believe?'

Faith brings glory to God

In John 11 we have the story of the death of Lazarus. Jesus allowed Lazarus to die because he had a plan to demonstrate his glory in a way that would not have happened if Lazarus had not died. Faith does not mean that all our circumstances will be instantly reversed as we might like them to be. But when the miracle does come it brings even greater glory to God, *because* of the apparent delay. When God wants to do something wonderful he starts with a difficult situation, even an impossible one. But he sometimes waits until the situation is so bleak, so irreversible, so desperate and so totally without human hope that when he works no one can boast in themselves about what they have received. That is why God often acts at the point of human hopelessness. When our efforts fail and we are at the point of desperation, he takes over. When we are completely void of all resources, and there is absolutely nothing that we can do to change our situation, we become willing to throw ourselves in desperation upon the mercy and the grace of God, and faith is free to operate.

When Jesus finally got to Bethany, Lazarus had already been dead for three days. Martha's tone was one of rebuke: 'Lord, if you had been here my brother would not have died.' Then Jesus said, 'Did I not tell you that if you believed you would see the glory of God.' Once again we are reminded that faith comes before seeing. Faith makes the invisible, visible. It is faith that brings the glory of God into a situation.

Faith enables mighty works

Hebrews 11 is faith's roll of honour. Without exception everyone listed there is described as demonstrating great deeds of faith as God's power was released in faith. These champions lived by faith. Faith dominated their choices, their actions, the course of their lives and in many cases, through them faith influenced the destiny of nations. That is what distinguishes true men and women of God from their unbelieving counterparts. They have a faith that accomplishes the mighty works of God.

Take the example of Noah who built an ark in a situation where boats were unknown. It was completely ludicrous, but faith enabled him to rise above the ridicule of the day and the cynicism of those around him to do something that had never been done before. And as a result of his obedience, God was able to bring about a new beginning in his purposes on the earth.

Perhaps an even more powerful example of obedient faith was Abraham. As a result of his obedience the whole nation of Israel was established and it was through that nation that God blessed the world. By faith Abraham was enabled to become a father even though Sarah was barren. By faith Abraham received that promise and we are blessed today by being part of that same experience. By faith Isaac was offered as a sacrifice when God tested him. Faith gives *us* the same ability to stand the tests of life. Those tests come to us almost on a daily basis and while faith is not an insurance policy against these things, it is an *assurance* policy throughout them, so that God's power is never in doubt.

To summarise, faith pleases God, makes the impossible possible, brings glory to God and enables mighty works to take place. We need men and women who are strong in faith, capable of achieving similarly great things today. This is what is frequently missing in the Christian Church today. Indeed, my purpose in writing this book is to challenge people to live as men and women of faith: people who will not put method before relationship or their ideas before God's will and God's purpose. Such men and women will simply believe God, take God at his Word, and act upon it that his will may be done effectively and powerfully on earth. My fervent prayer is that the kingdom of God may come through men and women who believe in *our* day.

4 Hearing the Word

Faith comes by hearing, and hearing by the Word of God (Romans 10:17).

In our walk with God, simplicity is the key: it is the hallmark of faith. Faith is simply believing God. It is not striving to believe, but comes as the supernatural working of God within us by his Word and his Spirit enabling us to believe. No matter how hard we try we can never produce faith by our own efforts. It begins when we hear God speak. This hearing of faith is not merely acknowledging that God has said something, but that he has spoken to us personally and intimately and so his Word begins to work deep within us.

Faith is a process

Faith begins with hearing the Word but it does not end there. It follows the full progression of the Word at work in our lives until the whole process of faith is complete. One way of looking at this is to think of faith as a chain with a number of interlocking and inter-relating links. As one link in the chain connects with another, so the process of faith unfolds. This process of faith is completed when we have an entire, unbroken chain of responses to the Word of God operating deep in our hearts. In order for the chain of faith to be complete, I have found that *seven links* must be in place. Each link has to do with our response to the Word at work in us. At every stage the Holy Spirit too is active, working with the Word, and empowering us to respond to God. We will be looking at each of these links in detail later on, but first, we begin with an overview of the whole faith process.

Seven vital links

Hearing the Word
Paul says in Romans 10:17, 'faith comes by hearing and hearing by the Word of God'. This means we must give careful attention to the Word of God. It is the seed from which a life of faith grows. Faith cannot operate outside of God's Word.

Believing the Word
Again we can turn to Romans 10, 'For it is with the heart one believes to righteousness, and with the mouth confession is made to salvation' (v 10). By 'believing' the Apostle means receiving the Word deep into our beings so that it takes root in our hearts, thus affecting the way we live the whole of our lives.

Confessing the Word
When faith is at work in our heart, it influences what we say and we begin to speak according to the Word of God. The promise of Romans 10:9 is that 'if you confess with your mouth, "Jesus is Lord", and believe in your heart that God raised him from the dead, you will be saved' (NIV).

Doing the Word
For every confession of faith there is corresponding

action that must accompany faith and complete it. This is confirmed in James 2:17, 'In the same way, faith by itself, if it is not accompanied by action, is dead' (NIV). Faith and appropriate actions work together (see James 2:22).

Standing firm on the Word

Faith has to be tested in order to develop and to mature, but that can only happen as we stand firm on the promises of God's Word. The Apostle James is always practical in his teaching, so again his words are valuable for our life of faith: 'because you know that the testing of your faith develops perseverance. Perseverance must finish its work so that you may be mature and complete, not lacking anything' (James 1:3–4 NIV). Peter also emphasises that faith is 'refined' by fire (that is, testings, trials and suffering) in 1 Peter 1:6–7.

Rejoicing in the Word

The true attitude of faith is reflected in a positive and buoyant outlook with genuine thanksgiving for what God has done, is doing and what he will yet do. Peter strikes this encouraging note in his first Epistle, 'whom having not seen you love. Though now you do not see Him, yet believing, you rejoice with joy inexpressible and full of glory' (1:8).

Persevering in the Word

Faith is rewarded when we continue to hold on to the truth of God's Word until it has been completely fulfilled. The writer of Hebrews says, 'Therefore do not cast away your confidence, which has great reward. For you have need of endurance, so that after you have done the will of God, you may receive the promise' (10:35–6; compare Hebrews 10:38 and 1 Peter 1:8–9).

Hearing with faith

The first link in the chain is 'hearing'. This sets the process of faith in motion. In the matter of faith, as in so many other things, how you begin is crucial. If we start off on the wrong foot we can so easily be out of step all the way through. Faith begins by giving God your attention, listening to him. It presupposes a ready ear and a willing heart. It means we take time with him and give him the opportunity to speak. Faith is conceived by the Word, like a seed sown deep into our lives. It often comes in the silence of our hearts as a still, small voice, as Christine discovered.

She was having difficulty with discipline in her class. The head had given her the toughest assignment in the school because he knew she was a confident and capable teacher. Her strong personality meant very few children got one over her, but this class was more than even she could cope with. They were particularly unruly and she never felt more hopeless and frustrated in all her eighteen years since leaving her home in West Africa. Usually, she would bounce back at any situation or obstacle in her way, but not this time. Matters grew worse, until she began to wonder if she was even going to lose her job. It was then she heard the voice of God. It came as a silent assurance along the lines of Scripture, 'in quietness and confidence shall be your strength' (Isaiah 30:15). This quiet voice inside grew in Christine, until it became a confident expectation that God would act. After a time some of the more disruptive pupils were moved to another class and she found she was able to work effectively with the rest.

It had not just been the result of her experience or competence as a teacher; God had worked for Christine. Faith has nothing to do with human striving or efforts: it is simply responding to God. That is the hallmark, etched into every link of this chain of faith. The pure gold of faith can carry no other inferior metal or impure substance. Faith joins itself to the flawless Word of God and must therefore from the beginning be carried in a purified heart. God has his way of purifying our hearts and refining our faith so that it will be as pure gold, but the hearing of faith sets us off in the right direction.

Hearing is the simple act of responding to what is being said. If God has not said it, then there can be no hearing and there will be no genuine faith. It is in the very nature of faith itself to focus on what God has said, not on our own ideas or desires for ourselves. Selfish faith is a contradiction. And yet some teaching on faith today has been narrowed down simply to getting things from God. This is the criticism that has been particularly levelled against charismatic Christians, but I have found that in all forms of Christianity the danger can be there, and we can soon be found living for ourselves and our comfort rather than for the glory of the Lord.

The importance of the 'cross-life'

In order for the seed to be productive, there first has to be fertile soil. The Word of God must be buried deep into hearts receptive and ready to let it bear fruit for God, without attempting to reap it for selfish ends. The incorruptible, ever-living seed of the Word cannot be perverted, changed or manipulated into something it was never intended to be.

This is why it is interesting to notice that, in the Apostle Paul's view, a life of faith begins with the cross: 'I have been crucified with Christ; it is no longer I who live, but Christ lives in me; and the life which I now live in the flesh I live by faith in the Son of God, who loved me and gave Himself for me' (Galatians 2:20). Until we can get to the place where we can say meaningfully, not just theoretically, that we have been crucified with Christ, we will not be fully released into a life of faith.

In order to live a life of faith, we have to be rescued from this present evil age and enter into the kingdom of God, and in doing so we are set free from a spirit of self-centredness. Having been set free from self by the power of God, we can then live our lives for him. And our prayers too become unselfish, concentrating on the things that bring God glory.

More specifically, our freedom comes through being crucified with Christ. Having died with Christ, we are now set free from those inner passions and desires that the Bible calls the 'flesh', as it says in Galatians 5:24, 'And those who are Christ's have crucified the flesh with its passions and desires.' In the same way Christ sets us free from the constraints and pressures of a world that seeks to squeeze us into its own mould. All this is vitally important for a life of faith. In fact Paul's prayer was 'God forbid that I should boast except in the cross of our Lord Jesus Christ, by whom the world has been crucified to me and I to the world' (Galatians 6:14). So if we are truly to live a life of faith we must first experience crucifixion which sets us free from being dominated by the world's attitudes. Only then are we able to follow God's desires rather than our self-centred demands.

But after crucifixion, what happens? Resurrection. If we have been crucified with Christ then we have also

been made alive with him. This same truth is expressed
in Galatians 2:20: 'I have been crucified with Christ;
nevertheless I live, yet not I, but Christ lives in me.'
Now we are beginning to move into the realm of faith.
Faith is experiencing the resurrection life and power
of Christ coming from within us, and is therefore the
lifestyle of all true Christians.

Faith is a relationship, not a formula. It is hearing
and obeying a Person, and is not about mechanics or
techniques. Some so-called 'faith techniques' seem to
make God out to be some kind of heavenly slot machine
or genie in a lamp, allowing us to live our lives as we
please, but ready to do our bidding when we need help.
Things have gone badly wrong when we begin to think
like that. Many books and faith messages sadly seem
only to emphasise laws, principles and steps, as if God
is somehow subject to these things. God is Personal,
he is the Divine Being, and is not simply some power
to be manipulated. A force, like electricity, can be
generated, stored and released according to the 'laws'
of electricity. But we cannot treat God like that. The
Bible teaches that God is not an impersonal force, an it,
a thing or a power. He's the wonderful Sovereign Lord
of all, and he wants *a relationship* with us. And this
relationship is built on personal trust, not mechanical
principles.

Faith, not striving

Faith comes from hearing the Word of God and is not
the product of human action or effort. That's why faith
is contrasted with works in the Bible. Works come
through human effort, but faith is the working of God.
So there are no techniques, magical faith formulae,
there are no invisible faith laws to which God is subject

and must bow. God has set in motion faith principles but we might just as soon tell God that he's subject to the law of gravity as tell him he's subject to laws of faith. God stands infinitely outside all his creation, both the physical world and the spiritual world. He can by choice, by his authority and his grace, break into the spiritual and physical order and bring about his miraculous power and the demonstration of his love. But he alone can do it. We cannot make him do it. God is not controlled by us. He is sovereign. He is not subject to anyone. The Creator is not controlled by the creature. We reject pagan religions for their relentless ritual and repetitive religious acts, so let us avoid being foolish enough to think that by pulling a few strings we can get God's attention and manipulate him around the performance of our wants and wishes.

The book of Galatians is all about the superiority of grace over law. The stark contrast is clearly portrayed in Galatians chapter 3 verses 11 and 12: 'But that no one is justified by the law in the sight of God is evident, for "the just shall live by faith." Yet the law is not of faith, but "the man who does them shall live by them."' Verse 11 shows that no one is justified before God by the law because the righteous will live by faith. Works have to do with man's efforts and energy, but faith has to do with the power and achievements of God. Verse 12 explains that works are of necessity based on law, not faith. What Paul is talking about here is men and women trying to manipulate God by religious faith and fervour. They think that as a result of these things, God is going to look down on our lives and be impressed. God isn't impressed like that. When it comes to our relationship with him, it's not a question of our good deeds or any effort on our part, it's a question of what God has already provided in the person of Jesus Christ his

Son. So we do not live by law, not even the laws
of faith.

A love relationship

Paul comes to the heart of the matter when he says,
'the life I live in the body I live by faith in the Son
of God who loved me and gave Himself for me.'
He is speaking about a life of faith that's based on
a relationship, of simple trust and obedience to the
Son of God, Jesus Christ. All of this comes as a result
of what he's done – the Son of God *who loved me and
gave himself for me.* This is the highest expression of
the love of God. John 3:16 speaks of God's love for the
world and Ephesians 5:27 speaks about Christ's love
for the *Church*. But Galatians 2:20 brings us an even
more personal revelation that the Son of God loved
me and gave himself for *me*. It's the realisation of
that truth that releases us into a life of faith. God *is*
favourably disposed towards us. He could never be
more in favour of us than he is now. He is totally,
100 per cent behind us and his grace is available to
lift us up, to strengthen us and to release us into his
best plan for our lives.

I began to worship in the church I now pastor in
1972. Through the years the consistent message that
the Lord has stressed from our pulpit is that God loves
us, he can change our life, and he can make us into
something special for him. Roger started attending the
church, having been referred to our Christian drug and
alcohol rehabilitation centre. His psychiatrist had sent
his files to help orientate the workers in the centre to
Roger's problems. They were the thickest files they had
ever seen. Everything that was in them seemed to say,
'Hopeless case'. But gradually Roger began to open up

to the Lord in a new way, and God began to put his life back together again. He was soon off all drugs and medication and later went on to enjoy a stable marriage, living a productive life in the community.

I've seen many hundreds of broken people like Roger coming and finding Christ. Drug addicts have been delivered. People have found wholeness in their lives despite some tragedy that has hit them. I've seen people blessed and set free in so many ways down through the years, and it is all because the Spirit touched their lives through the simple message of the grace and love of Jesus.

The Spirit of faith

As we have seen, faith arises out of our relationship with Christ, but how do we relate to Christ? What does it mean to have Christ living in us? Have you ever thought about that? Where is Jesus now physically? He is seated at the right hand of the Father, so how can he also be living in us? The answer is by the Holy Spirit. So when Paul says, 'the life I live now in the flesh I live by faith in the Son of God who loved me and gave himself for me', he is speaking about the living presence of Christ in our lives through the Holy Spirit who empowers us and equips us for everyday living. Faith is not about human effort but it has everything to do with the operation of the Holy Spirit.

This should not surprise us. If faith comes by hearing the Word, then the Holy Spirit has to be involved. Jesus said, 'The words that I speak to you are spirit and they are life' (John 6:63). Where you have the Word, you also have the Spirit. The Word of God is the breath of his lips, given by the inspiration of the Holy Spirit. The Spirit and the Word belong together.

That is why a life of faith is also a Spirit-filled life.
Stephen was a man 'full of faith and the Holy Spirit'
(Acts 6:5). True faith is produced by the power of the
Holy Spirit working in us alongside the Word of God.
It is the Holy Spirit who enables us to hear the Word
spoken to us. He gives us the power to respond in
faith. He keeps our faith alive, as we embrace his
presence in our lives. He is the 'Spirit of faith' (2
Corinthians 4:13). All this is far from the common
substitutes of faith. Faith is not based in the human
intellect, the emotions or even the human will. These
are soulish, psychological forms of faith. They are not
real, but are man-made substitutes. True faith includes
the mind, emotions and the will, but is not rooted in
these areas. Faith operates out of the human spirit as
the Word is ignited by the Holy Spirit working in us.

We must all be ready to hold out for the genuine
spiritual working of the Word in our hearts by faith.
Remember all that God does on the earth is done
through believing people, not just a few great heroes
of faith who stand head and shoulders above everyone
else. The whole believing community of God's people
must move forward in faith to fulfil the will of God.
We need to open our ears and hearts to the truth of
the Word and respond to the new dynamic of the Holy
Spirit in us. We need to know Jesus as the 'author
and the finisher of our faith' (Hebrews 12:2), not by
struggling and striving through our own efforts but by
taking his hand and trusting him as he leads us by his
Spirit into the life of faith.

No faith substitutes

So far we've seen that faith comes by hearing God's
Word, and that this is only possible through the Holy

Spirit. No one can produce it, and if it can be produced by us, it is a substitute that is not of God. If we can switch it on and switch it off, we can be sure it is not of God. We don't control the Holy Spirit; the Holy Spirit controls us.

This brings me to an important word of warning that is necessary in today's society where there is so much spiritual opposition to the true work of the Holy Spirit. One of the ways that Satan opposes the work of God is by counterfeiting the genuine work of the Holy Spirit. The devil even offers a counterfeit faith which depends on false power. This power comes from demonic forces operating through the occult. The devil offers occult techniques from astrology to witchcraft which are means of manipulating the spirit realm. Here at once we see the difference between the genuine manifestation of God and that of demonic spirits. Every spirit that allows itself to be controlled and manipulated is occultic, counterfeit and not of God. Techniques of sorcery, positive thinking and mind science all work basically the same way, and the source of their power is the occult. We need to be able to discern between counterfeit spirits and the true spirit of faith. Let us examine how we can do that.

Here are the signs of false faith:

1 The promise of power on demand is occultic. We can't demand anything from God. Any kind of spiritual power that doesn't insist on the motive of love for Christ, or where motive is not important is not of God.

2 Anything that reduces spiritual power to impersonal forces is not of God. Faith comes out of a relationship with Jesus as we walk in holiness by the Holy Spirit.

3 Anything that teaches us techniques of accessing the spirit realm is occultic and is not of God.

4 Anything that relies on the techniques of mind control, the 'science of the mind' or our inner potential leans so dangerously to the occult that no Christian should even touch it.

5 Anything that offers slick technologies, formulae, mechanisms, techniques through which spiritual powers are said to operate is not of God.

6 Any kind of unbiblical channelling of spiritual power through physical objects and places, through special acts and rituals, special times and seasons is occultic. God is accessible by faith in Jesus Christ any time of the day, month, week or year simply by faith in Jesus Christ. We don't have to perform certain rituals, have magical words or formulae said over us.

7 Anything that rejects the reality of the material world and emphasises the so-called 'higher reality' of the spiritual world is not of God. God created the world and he made it good and he will redeem even this physical creation. It is his Word that is paramount.

8 Anything that teaches us that we can create our own reality by using spiritual laws or powers is not of God.

9 Any conviction or belief that is based on man's ideas, human philosophy or human intellect is inadequate. Man's opinions cannot be a substitute for God's revelation, neither is mere head-knowledge of God's Word. This is soulish, intellectual faith, and is not true faith.

10 Any approach to faith that does not genuinely lead to greater knowledge of and dependence on the person of Jesus Christ, and his atoning work on the cross, is a counterfeit approach.

Those who have been involved in any of the practices and approaches to spiritual matters outlined above should immediately renounce and reject them. But, do not fear, there is deliverance in the name of Jesus. As we confess our wrongful involvement, we can be cleansed and set free by the power of the blood of Jesus.

All these things point to the presence of a faith that is not genuine. But on the other hand, we can discern genuine faith, because it *confesses the person of Christ.* Not *a* Christ, one of many, but *the* Christ who has come in the flesh in the person of Jesus. Genuine faith confesses that Jesus gave his life as a sacrifice on the cross. When Jesus shed his blood he was paying the price of the sins of mankind and opening the way for us to receive the blessing of God. Only by the blood of Jesus Christ can we enter in. Genuine faith confesses and acknowledges that Jesus Christ has been raised from the dead and that Jesus Christ is Lord.

Not only does genuine faith confess the person of Christ, but genuine faith also submits to the person of Christ, in simple obedience and total dependence upon him. Genuine faith lives for this one thing alone, and that is to see the glory of Christ, not self. While all of us, including myself, fall short of this perfect, or mature faith, it is our desire to move more and more into the purity of the faith of God.

To summarise this chapter: we have seen that faith comes by hearing God's Word in the power of the Holy Spirit. God wants us to live by faith. Not just to reach a few notable high spots at infrequent intervals, but to have a whole lifestyle of faith. In order for this to be a reality in our experience, we need to appreciate that faith is a process which must be completed. It is a relationship in which we die to our own desires and follow Christ by his Spirit. And in particular, we die to any attempt to manipulate God which can lead to a dangerous substitute for true faith. In the next chapter we'll see how faith is not just *hearing* the Word, it's *believing* it too.

5   Believing the Word of Faith

He has given us His very great and precious promises (2 Peter 1:4 NIV).

God wants us to be doers of the Word, not just hearers. However, we cannot be either without faith. I have been stressing that it is our responsibility to believe God and to grow in faith before him. God is looking for men and women of faith who will rise above the climate of unbelief around them and do exploits for him. But God is not only looking for believing individuals, he is also searching for believing churches. God wants us to grow into believing communities, so that his purposes may also be fulfilled corporately in society, and not just personally in our own lives.

One of the most desperate challenges we are facing in the world today is the AIDS epidemic. But I came across a church where the Christian community is making an impact by faith. It was in Brooklyn, New York and the pastor introduced me to a young black girl whose mother, who had been a drug addict, had died of AIDS. The family who had been caring for the mother took her in. It was inevitable that the little girld should be HIV positive, and when the tests were done, their fears proved correct. But the church refused to give in. They are a believing community and so the whole church went to prayer. After a time the girl was taken back to the doctor and, after several repeated tests, was declared free from HIV. God had answered the persistent prayers of the community. Not everyone that has AIDS gets healed in this church, but like so many loving Christian communities all around the world, they continue to care for people with AIDS. Their faith is not in an aggressive evangelism alone but also in compassionate caring.

I have also been emphasising the Bible's teaching that faith comes as a result of God's grace at work in our lives. A paraphrase of Romans 4:16 would read, 'the promise comes by faith so that it may be by grace and may be guaranteed', and it's this guarantee that encourages me, because I know that if the strength of my faith depends upon my personality, my personal righteousness or my own ability, there is no guarantee at all. However, our faith is not in ourselves; it is in the Son of God who loved us and gave himself for us. And so faith comes into our lives as a result of God's grace. But now does it come? How does God's grace work faith in us? Faith comes from the promises of God. It is his Word that produces faith.

The Word of faith

Many people have a rather vague view of faith. To such people, faith is simply the act of believing, and the content of faith is not really important; it is up to the individual. We are to:d that it doesn't matter *what* you believe, only *that* you believe. It is sincerity that counts. This approach to faith is extremely common having been popularised by the media, the culture and the music of our day. There is a line from a song in the very successful West End musical *Joseph and his Amazing Technicolour Dreamcoat* which epitomises this view of faith. It says, 'any dream will do'; but that is *not* true, any dream will *certainly not* do.

Joseph dreamed *God's* dreams and we need God's dreams for our lives. The whole world is given over to its own dreams and its own ideas. We are not free simply to invent the content of our faith; faith does not operate like that. God has spoken, and we either believe or disbelieve what he says. When we reject his Word, all we have left are our thoughts and opinions. In the time of Judges, each person 'did what was right in his own eyes'. That's why society then was in a mess. The same is true today.

We must begin to dream God's dreams, to see God's visions, to discern God's thoughts, hear his Word and to see his burden for our lives individually and corporately. *His* dream will outstrip *our* dreams. You think you've got plans for your life – wait until you hear God's plans! Every one of his plans is based on the thousands of promises that God has spoken, written and infallibly recorded in his Word, the Scriptures. So we need to line up with the Word of God, and lay hold of the things that God has said, because that is the Word of faith.

The promises

2 Peter 1 tells us that God has given us 'exceedingly great and precious promises' (v 4). And these come to us 'by the righteousness of our God and Saviour, Jesus Christ' (2 Peter 1:1). The promises have to do with the things that God has accomplished for us through Christ who is the 'author and finisher of our faith'. He is also its object and content. People hold to all kinds of beliefs, common in today's world, but biblical faith is not about ordinary beliefs, or even specifically religious beliefs. Biblical faith is about *the* faith, as it has been revealed in Jesus Christ. Only through Jesus

Christ has God made his blessings available; they are only available through 'the righteousness of our God and Saviour Jesus Christ'.

God has never revealed himself in isolation from his people, but always shows himself to be what he is in a relationship of love. At various times in history God has revealed his character and love towards us through his names. These names are not abstract labels but revelations of who God is and what he promises to do for us.

Jehovah (Yahweh): 'I am who I am' or, 'I will be what I will be' (Exodus 3:14,15), is the name of God by which he promises to act for his people. Just as he promised to deliver his people Israel from the hand of the oppressor in Egypt, so he promises to set us free in order to experience his blessings. This name is a blanket promise for him to be to us whatever we need him to be to fulfil his covenant of love.

El-Shaddai (God Almighty): The God who met Abram at the point of his human weakness and desperation will meet us when we need his almighty power (Genesis 17:1). God transformed both Abram, making him Abraham, the father of a multitude, and his circumstances (childlessness) in order to fulfil his covenant purposes. In the same way God promises to transform both us and our circumstances so that they conform to his best will for our lives.

Jehovah-Shammah (The Lord is There): The exiles who were to return home to Judah after the exile were promised in Ezekiel 48:30–5 that they would not be alone. God himself would be with them and when they returned they would find him there. When we step out in obedience to the Lord we also will discover we are not alone. God promises to be with us in all situations and circumstances as our ever-present Helper.

Jehovah-Jireh (The Lord who Provides): Just as

Abraham knew that the Lord himself would provide a lamb for the sacrifice he had commanded (Genesis 22:8,14) so we have the equal assurance that God will give us everything we need to obey him. He will provide for our every need: physical, emotional and spiritual.

El-Roy (The God who Sees): God looked down and saw the lonely Hagar who had been cast out of Abraham's household together with her son Ishmael (Genesis 16:13). God sees and acts on behalf of the lonely, the helpless and the disregarded.

Jehovah-Nissi (The Lord my Banner): God gave a remarkable victory to Israel in the famous battle against the Amalekites. As Moses' hands were upheld on the hill top, Joshua and the army of Israel prevailed in the valley. God promises to lift up our hands when we are weary in the fight and strengthen us in his battle. We have the promise of complete victory.

Jehovah-Tsidkenu (The Lord our Righteousness): This is the name by which Messiah, the Christ, was to be known (Jeremiah 23:6), and by which Jerusalem was to be called (Jeremiah 33:16). It is the means by which we shall be justified, or declared righteous. God promises to credit us with the righteousness of Christ who died our death on the cross so that we might receive the provision of God's righteousness in our life.

Jehovah-Shalom (The Lord is Peace): This was the name of Gideon's altar that he built after he had seen the angel of the Lord (Judges 6:24). Gideon was called as God's mighty man of valour in order to break the oppression of the Midianites. God promises to release us from the oppression of the enemy and to stop his intimidation. We have no need to fear: God's peace is with us.

Jehovah-Rophe (The Lord, the Healer): The Lord

promises to be Israel's healer as she walks in obedience to him (Exodus 15:26). God has not changed, it is still his nature to heal. We too can claim healing from him. Christ has fulfilled every obligation of the law of God on our behalf and has carried the curse of sickness on the cross.

Jehovah-M'kaddesh (The Lord who Makes Holy): The Lord is a holy God and he makes his people holy (Leviticus 20:8). He sanctifies us, sets us apart for him and gives us his holiness within so that we can rise above the power of sin and live pure lives before him.

Jehovah-Rohi (The Lord my Shepherd): As King David knew from his time as the shepherd boy on the hills of Bethlehem, shepherds care for their sheep. The Lord is our Shepherd, the one who looks after us, guides us, protects us, feeds us and provides for all our needs so that we will never lack (Psalm 23:1).

Only in Jesus Christ

Because Jesus has so perfectly accomplished God's salvation for us, God has given him a name which is above every name (Philippians 2:9). It is in this name, and only in this name, that we can now come and enjoy the promises of God, as Paul says: 'For all the promises of God in Him are Yes, and in Him Amen, to the glory of God through us' (2 Corinthians 1:20).

God can only bless us through the righteousness of Jesus Christ; we have none of our own. Jesus Christ lived sinlessly, perfectly fulfilling the righteousness of God, and that righteousness now is made available to us freely through his sacrificial death on the cross. Jesus lived a righteous life and yet died a sinner's death. His death on the cross was a sacrifice offered for the sins of the whole world. The cross of Jesus Christ is God's key which unlocks the door into the storehouse of God's goodness. As a result of the death of Jesus Christ, and the resurrection that followed, we have access to the blessing of God. Every promise is secured by faith in Jesus Christ.

Worthy to receive?

Some of us are struggling to believe for something specific from God, and we wonder whether we deserve to receive it, and the Lord says, 'No! You don't. But it's not on the basis of what you deserve, it's on the basis of my love for you!' Faith gives us access into the grace of God and the basis of it all is the atonement. It's the death of Jesus Christ. Grace is not cheap, and neither is faith, but we don't have to pay the bill: Jesus has paid it for us all! There isn't any more glorious news than that anywhere in the world. The sublime truth is this: the way to God is open *now*, for all who believe.

Apostolic faith

Having removed the first barrier in the way of receiving from God – our unworthiness – Peter destroys another lie of the enemy which says, 'You'll never have enough faith to receive the blessing of God.' What a tragedy, that the promised blessings which have been so freely made available to us in Christ, should now be withheld from our experience through unbelief. And that is where the devil is most active. He convinces us that it would require far greater faith than *we* could ever possess to see our circumstances overturned and the promises fulfilled in our lives.

But the Apostle Peter says, 'Through the righteousness of our God and Saviour Jesus Christ you have received a faith as precious as ours' (2 Peter 1:1 NIV). We have obtained 'like precious faith', with the apostles. We have received the same kind of faith that was at work in them. What was possible for them, is possible for us. And to whom is the Apostle Peter speaking? To some special class of super-believers? No! He is speaking to ordinary Christians like you and me.

Sometimes we think that the Bible characters who achieved great things for God are somehow in a different category from the rest of us, that they really had what it takes. But as for us – we could never attain to the levels of faith and power that they did. We have to live some kind of inferior, second-class Christianity. But this is simply not true. The apostles did have a special call: they were Christ's first generation ambassadors, who were called to special levels of power and divine inspiration in their time. But we are called to be the apostolic community of today. We need God's power, today. We need to receive help for our lives, strength for our souls and provision for our bodies. The promises of the Bible are just as true for today as they were for people in Bible times. Jesus Christ has not changed; he is 'the same yesterday, today and for ever' (Hebrews 13:8), and God has given us exactly the same faith that was at work in the early Church in order to see the same things happen today.

Nothing is impossible for the Church of our generation. God is restoring us into a fully apostolic Church. That involves having the true apostolic faith which has been passed down the generations through the Word of God. When we enter into a right relationship with God through faith in Jesus Christ, we stand in the line of succession of those who had the same faith that was present in the apostles; similarly, the same Spirit that rested on Peter and Paul rests upon us. Peter and Paul are dead: they've gone. But Jesus Christ is still living and working on this earth, by his Holy Spirit.

The mighty works of Christ did not finish with the apostles who were mere instruments of the same anointing that has been poured out on *this* generation. Why then does the present-day Church seem so powerless by comparison with the New Testament Church? It is because we fail to grasp the promises of God. We must believe them, growing in our experience of them, to the point where we fully demonstrate them as the body of Christ, God's agent in the world today. Encourage yourself by repeating the phrase, 'I have the same faith that was in the apostles of Christ', to yourself. With that we can begin to do something. This faith gives us access to his very great and precious promises. Let's now look a little more closely at the scope of these promises.

Everything we need

His divine power has given to us all things that pertain to life and godliness, through the knowledge of Him who called us by glory and virtue, by which have been given to us exceedingly great and precious promises (2 Peter 1:3–4).

As a result of the work of Jesus Christ, *God has made provision for our every conceivable need*. There isn't anything that we will face that God has not already provided for; and it's all found in the Word of God. There are promises for every kind of condition, for needs of every description and for every area of life.

God has made promises for our personal life, for the health and healing of our body, and for our home and family. There are promises for our well-being and prosperity. Biblical prosperity is having more than enough provision for your own needs so that you can minister to other people's needs. There is no need that we have ever experienced or ever will experience, other than that which God has already provided for through the promises of his Book. And with every one of these promises comes the power to fulfil them in our life.

Life and godliness

That's why Peter says that through his divine power God has given us everything we need for *life* and for *godliness*. Those two words are very important for our faith. The word life is the Greek word *zoe* which is used frequently of spiritual life. It's not *bios* biological life, but *zoe* spiritual life. The Word of God releases within us power to live the life God provides. It is even explained by Peter as 'participating in the divine nature' (2 Peter 1:4 NIV). We have the life of God living in us, activating us, and us moving within. This new life is called being 'born again' – a much maligned, but nevertheless biblical term. Everything that we need for the promotion and development of this new life from God is found in the promises of Scripture.

The second word, godliness, relates to the *outworking* of this spiritual life. God has given us *zoe*, spiritual life, and that life is to be outworked in every area before him. That's what godliness is, a fundamental disposition towards God which is reflected in all we do. It means that we are godly on the way to the bus, and godly when the bus doesn't come. It means we are godly when the bus is full so that when it does come, we can't get on it! It means that we are godly at home, at work and at recreation. It means that we live the whole of our life before God who sees our activities twenty-four hours a day.

God's eyes are upon us each moment of every day, and his power is sufficient to cover every area of our life. All this is packed into the promises of God's book. It is 'through *these promises* we participate in the divine nature and escape from the corruption that's in the world through lusts or through desires' (2 Peter 1:4). The promises of faith enable us to do two things in particular, to escape from the old, and to participate in the new. It's rather like the children of Israel when they escaped from Egypt. They had to come out of that land of bondage in order to enter into the promised land of Canaan. By faith Moses parted the Red Sea and delivered them from Egypt, and by faith Joshua led those same people into their inheritance in Canaan. Coming out was in order to enter in.

In the same way, not only have we to come out, but we must also enter in to God's promises. We have to turn away from sin and embrace righteousness. We must turn away from our failure and negative past and begin to live the life of God. That's what faith is all about. Moving forward day by day, with our back resolutely set against the former way of life, taking possession of *all* the promises of God. The full potential God has for us lies before us like the promised land, waiting for us to rise up and possess it as our inheritance. I believe the Lord will one day show us, alongside what we attained on the earth, how much we could have attained. How wonderful it would be for the Lord to be able to say on that day, 'This is all that I gave you, and this is all that you took', and for us to see that we have received everything that he made available for us. I know that's a tall order, but I'm sure it's something worth reaching for.

Obtaining the promises

So God's promises are the *vital source of faith*. It operates on the promises of the Word, and we must learn how to lay hold of them all.

Find the promises
If you don't find the promises, how are you going to act on them? How can we take hold of the promises if we don't know them? Therefore, you must be searching the Word of God daily, recording biblical promises. There are lots of ways of doing this, but it's best to go straight to the Word of God for yourself. Highlight the promises in your Bible, get them into your heart and claim them that way. Find the promises and know them.

Believe the promises
Finding them is one thing, believing them is an altogether different matter. We may have coloured our Bible completely, cover to cover, and underlined every promise in ball-point or felt-tip pen, but if it is only a highlighting of the texts on the pages, it means nothing. To believe the promises means *they have to be highlighted in your heart*.

Fulfil the conditions
This is, for us all, the difficult bit. God wants us to align our hearts with his will so that his will can operate in our lives. It's not just a question of quoting texts and saying, 'Lord, there it is, you've got to bless me now, because it says so here.' Without fulfilling the conditions, you cannot qualify for the promise. Check

out the conditions, fulfil them and the promise will be yours.

Receive the promises

While I am outlining the principles of the promises one by one, don't forget that you are receiving from God, not from a slot machine. Faith is a relationship. I have heard people say, 'I've found the promise, I've believed God's Word, and I'm fulfilling the conditions but I haven't received.' Faith is not automatic; there are many factors at work. One of them is our overall spiritual development. God knows what we need and when we need it. Also, there is the element of testing. Faith must be tested to prove whether it is genuine. Then there is also the opposition from the enemy, our adversary the devil. We have to press our case in opposition to Satan. Although the devil is already defeated he remains aggressively persistent, and he can outstrip the persistence of the average Christian. He can usually hinder our prayers more times than we are willing to pray them. The evidence of that is possibly in our own life right now, when after a period of time we have stopped asking God, or believing him for certain things. We've allowed the enemy's discouragement to come against us and to distract us to the point of giving up altogether. Don't ever give up. God is faithful. Don't let the devil beat you with determination. If he's determined, be more determined, and keep on until you have *received* the promise.

Fule and Ruth, a middle-aged couple, were longing for a child. They had prayed to God for many years and yet there seemed to be no answer. The doctors had not given them much hope of ever having a child and had even begun to counsel them to think of other options. Fule tried to comfort Ruth, 'Don't torture yourself any

longer. We have each other. Let's just accept that and
be happy.' But Ruth said, 'The Lord promised me I
would have children.' She was very definite. God had
spoken to her many years before and she had held on to
that word ever since then. At times the situation seemed
so desperate that she almost gave up hope altogether.
And then one Sunday during the church service God
spoke to her heart: 'Your prayer has been answered',
he said. Ruth went home full of joy. It was as if she
had conceived already. Just under two years later she
gave birth to a beautiful baby boy. Her determination
in faith prevailed.

It stands written

My emphasis in this chapter is the Word of faith, and
I have been at pains to point out that the operation of
faith in our lives is not cold or clinical; rather it is the
outworking of the relationship we have with the Lord,
by his Spirit. And this can also be seen from the way
the Word of God works in our lives. The Word of
God operates in you spiritually and not mechanically.
The Word carries within itself the power for its own
fulfilment. God has spoken once through the promises;
he does not have to speak a second time in order for us
to believe, we must believe the Word, already spoken.
But the way all this happens is a process involving
a two-way relationship of divine activity and human
response.

God's Word, spoken and written, is a living Word.
It is alive and active, as it says in Hebrews 4:12:
'For the Word of God is living and powerful, and
sharper than any two-edged sword.' The Scripture is
not a dead letter written long ago, but is every bit as
real, and powerfully active as when first spoken and

recorded in written form. God's Word is incorruptible, it lives and abides for ever (1 Peter 1:23), it stands firm, settled for ever in heaven (Psalm 119:89). In the same way what is written stands, on the earth too. That is, after all, the burning issue. God's Word which has absolute authority in heaven has equal power on the earth. When New Testament writers quote from the Old Testament, they often use a tense in the original Greek, which clearly expresses this truth. They do not merely say, 'It was written', or 'God said', implying something that only happened long ago. They say, 'It stands written', or 'God says', showing that the Word of God given long ago still speaks and is active today. Faith takes hold of the 'now' Word of God, it operates in the present realm reaching for the present activity of the Word, in the world today.

When I became a Christian, I heard the Word of God. I have no real recollection of hearing the Gospel on any occasion other than at the time I accepted Jesus. But when I think about it, I can look back on situations where I must have heard the message preached. But I don't actually remember hearing the Gospel, until the day I responded from the heart to the Truth, and became born again. There is a big difference between hearing and responding to what you hear. We can hear the Word in an outward fashion and not take it in – there is no conviction attached to what we hear. But then there comes a time when the Word is preached and something different happens. Suddenly we hear, with the internal ears of our heart; and hearing, we respond.

But what are we responding to? It is not merely the Word, but the Word at work in our hearts, coming to us with the conviction of the Spirit. It is not just the Word touching the superficial levels of our personality, but the Word penetrating with the razor-sharp precision of a surgeon's knife, finding and healing the deepest parts of our lives. The Word penetrates and lays bare our most intimate thoughts and intentions and operates at the deepest level of the human spirit, 'piercing even to the division of soul and spirit, and of joints and marrow, and is a discerner of the thoughts and intents of the heart' (Hebrews 4:12). This is no mere mechanical 'claiming of the promises', but an interaction with the living Word of God, allowing it full and free access into the deepest parts of our human personality. This is only possible through the activity of the Holy Spirit.

Logos and rhema

All this leads naturally on to the distinction that is often drawn between two Greek words, *logos* and *rhema*. Both these words mean basically the same thing, '*word*', and are often used interchangeably in the New Testament. However, in some contexts there is a distinction between them. Some Bible teachers on faith use this distinction to teach a very important principle, that faith arises out of *rhema* not *logos*. Vine, the great Bible scholar, in his *Expository Dictionary of New Testament Words*, writes '*Logos* denotes the expression of thought. *Rhema* denotes that which is spoken.' Because God's thoughts and character do not change, *logos* is readily used of God's general Word. It's the *general expression of his Word*, but *rhema* is his *particular Word*, his Word revealed to us and active in us personally. So, in order for faith to operate, the *rhema* must be released.

That's what Romans 10:17 teaches. It says faith comes from hearing God's message, and hearing from the *rhema* of God, or the message of God, or the Word of Christ *to you personally*. So in order for a promise to be released in true faith in our lives we must hear it not just as *logos* but as *rhema*. Not just as God's general Word to everybody, but as God's specific Word to you. That makes all the difference. Take for example the Scripture verse, 'God so loved the world that He gave His only begotten Son so whoever believes in Him should not perish but have everlasting life' (John 3:16). That is God's general Word for everyone. Who does God love? Everyone. However, it is only when you realise that within that general Word to everyone, there is also a specific Word for you, that you enjoy the benefits of the promise. *Faith operates at the level of the personal, not the general.* When we hear from that verse God saying, 'I loved you so much that I gave my Son for you, and when you believe, you will receive eternal life', when we hear it that way, suddenly faith is released in our hearts and we say, 'Yes, I want that love!' It's exactly the same for all transactions of faith. We know that Jesus died on the cross and bore in his own body our sin and our suffering. We know that also Jesus paid the ultimate price that releases all God's promises to us. *Rhema* is the Word, spoken to us, personally, not as an ancient Word of long ago, but a 'now' Word working inside us.

Rhema is the Word that brings forth faith. It is fruitless just to take God's Word externally. It cannot help you any more than you can be helped by reading your prescription from your local doctor. You must fulfil the prescription, obtain the medicine from the chemist, and then take the medicine. In the same way you must let the Word of God work deeply in you. Mechanical claiming of the promises, or simply reciting Scriptures with your mouth is not faith. Faith is taking the Word, hearing it as it is, God speaking to you now, and then feeding on that Word as if it were your very food. That's what Jesus meant when he said,

'It is written, "Man shall not live by bread alone, but by every word that proceeds from the mouth of God"' (Matthew 4:4). The true food of faith is the living Word (*rhema*) that *is proceeding* from the mouth of God.

Surely it's time for us to stop only hearing the Word with the outer ear, and to begin to hear with the inner ear of faith. We are all too familiar with the Scriptures, and yet know very little of their power in our lives. There are vast areas in God's land of promise, revealed in the Bible, that we haven't even begun to explore, let alone inherit. We are keen not to be presumptuous and chase what is *not* promised but are even more likely to be contemptuous in disregarding what he *has* promised. We must extend the borders of faith. The promises lead us forward to receive, not only the initial benefits of salvation and freedom from sin, but also the blessings that cover the rest of life. Let us go on to receive those *rhema* words from the Lord for the health and healing of our body, for our finances, for the strength of our spiritual lives and for the *whole range* of God's promises to us in his Word.

6 Confessing the Word

*For with the heart one believes to righteousness,
and with the mouth confession is made to salvation* (Romans 10:10).

Confession is an essential part of faith. In fact, faith
and confession are inseparable: you cannot have one
without the other. Psalm 19:14 says, 'Let the words
of my mouth and the meditation of my heart be
acceptable in Your sight, O Lord my strength and
my Redeemer.' God said to the young Joshua when
he took over as leader of Israel from Moses, 'This
Book of the Law shall not depart from your mouth,
but you shall meditate in it day and night, that you
may observe to do according to all that is written in
it. For then you will make your way prosperous, and
then you will have good success' (Joshua 1:8). So
God's instruction was, 'Don't fail to have my word in
your mouth.' What does this mean? It has to do with
confessing the Word of God.

The power of the tongue

Many of us will know from the Bible that the tongue
has great power. In James 3, it is compared to the
rudder that steers a massive ship and also a spark
that has the potential to burn down a mighty forest.
James says, 'the tongue is a fire, a world of iniquity.

The tongue is so set among our members that it defiles the whole body, and sets on fire the course of nature; and it is set on fire by hell' (James 3:6). Evil speaking is the negative aspect of the tongue when it is not yielded to the control of the Holy Spirit. Notice how destructive it can be.

The tongue rightly used

But the tongue can also be used constructively as a weapon for the glory of God. That's why the Book of Proverbs says, 'Death and life are in the power of the tongue, and those who love it will eat its fruit' (18:21). We have the capacity to speak words of encouragement that build people up and minister life, or we can speak negative and destructive words that tear down. Words give expression to our inner thoughts and communicate to others. What we say can influence them and help shape the world around us. Therefore, as Christians, we should surrender our tongues to the Holy Spirit's control and be careful never to let hurtful or damaging words out of our mouths. Our words can kill. They can destroy what we should rather be building. Even our prayers can be hindered through our negative speaking. Faith can be undermined by the words of our lips. We can put doubt in other people's minds by what we say, and we can enforce our own unbelief through habitual evil thinking or negative talking. Words are not just sounds, but carry the meaning and intention of their source, the speaker, and have great power.

God's Words of course have superlative power. Hebrews 4:12 says the Word of God is both living and active. God never speaks an idle Word. He always speaks intentionally in order to fulfil a purpose of his. In Isaiah 55:10–11 God says, 'For as the rain comes down, and the snow from heaven, and do not return there, but water the earth, and make it bring forth and bud, that it may give seed to the sower and bread to the eater, so shall My word be that goes forth from My mouth; it shall not return to Me void, but it shall accomplish what I please, and it shall prosper in the thing for which I sent it.' *So when God speaks, things happen.* For example, in the beginning God said, 'Let there be light', and there was light. He speaks and it is done. He never outspeaks his capacity or his ability to fulfil his Word. Many of us do. We say great things but are totally incapable of fulfilling them, but God always has power to do what he says.

An example of this is the building of the temple in Jerusalem by King Solomon. The promise of the Lord was that Solomon was going to build the temple in place of his father, David. When Solomon completed the work, he prayed a prayer of dedication and said, 'Lord . . . you have both spoken with your mouth and fulfilled it with your hand' (2 Chronicles 6:15). God has power to fulfil with his hand what he promises with his mouth, and by faith we need to grasp the unlimited power of the Word of God.

The Word of God in you

By faith we lay hold of the power of God's Word, believe it and respond to what God has said. God has already spoken; he has given us his Word, the Bible. But having the Bible in our hand, by itself, is not going to stimulate faith. We could take the Bible and put it in as many hospitals as we like but nobody is going to get healed just because the Bible is there. Until people read the Bible and begin to believe it, the Word will not affect their lives at all. Every promise of salvation is wasted unless we *believe*. Every promise of healing is wasted unless we *receive* that Word. The Word of faith is not God speaking his Word, but it is *you* speaking his Word. The Apostle Paul explained this when he said that, having heard the message of faith, we must confess with our lips that Jesus Christ is Lord and believe in our heart that God raised him from the dead, and then we shall be saved (Romans 10:8–10). Without confession, there is no salvation because genuine faith always leads to genuine confession.

Richard, a rebellious young man, dropped out of school and left home at the age of 16. The next few years found him getting deeper and deeper into drugs and the underworld. He became a drug dealer in order to support his own drug habit and lived a life of crime until the police finally caught up with him and he ended up in prison. Bored, with plenty of time on his hands, he picked up a copy of the New Testament that had been placed in his cell. He began to read, bemused by the unfamiliar language of the King James Bible. But soon he found the words compelling and something stirred in his heart. As he read on, he became aware that he had changed; his whole belief system had been transformed. Immediately he began to confess Christ to his fellow inmates. 'It's like picking up a live electric cable!' he said. Faith had begun to explode in his heart and it was beginning to show in his life.

Drawing from the Book of Deuteronomy, Paul says the Word of faith 'is near you, in your mouth and in your heart' (Romans 10:8). It was the Word that Paul was proclaiming and that the Christians were confessing. The Word of faith must be preached and received; it must also be believed and confessed. The Word of faith is God's Word that we proclaim and confess. It is my firm conviction that God's Word through my mouth has as much power as God's Word through his mouth! That's what true confession is. The word 'confess' literally means 'to say the same things as', and when we confess the Word of faith, we are saying the same things as God says in his Word. Confession is verbal agreement with the Word of God, but for it to be true confession, the agreement must come also from the heart.

Stephanie was devastated when she discovered her husband who had been away on business was no longer living as a Christian should. They had been married two years and were to all intents and purposes very happy. Charles had been promoted in the company, but it meant being away from home much more than before. Stephanie refused to accept the rumours of his drinking and immorality, until she found out the truth for herself.

'I cannot accept it. This is not the Charles I married', she said, but the situation got worse. Her family and friends could not see any future in the marriage, but Stephanie would not give in. She kept the Charles she had known in her heart and prayed to God for a miracle. She was blond with blue-grey eyes and fine features, although now she felt ugly and worthless; but she would not let go of the man she had married, trying hard not to reject the man he had now become.

Day by day, almost without knowing it, and certainly not as a faith technique, she began to declare, 'Charles is not the man I see. He is a good Christian husband.' She never stopped believing in him and in God's promise to her that he would come back. Months and even years went by, but Stephanie kept on saying, 'Charles will be back. God is going to give me back the man I married.' That is what she believed in her heart. Not as the wishful desires of a woman who could not accept that she had lost her husband, but a genuine heart conviction from the Holy Spirit coming from her desperate times in God's presence in prayer. Her faith confession was based on true faith conviction in her heart. Charles did come back and despite the pain, through forgiveness and reconciliation, the marriage was completely restored.

True confession arises from within. It's not just a question of what you say, but what you believe in your heart. What is in the heart will be reflected by what you say, as the scripture has it, 'The word is near you, in your mouth and in your *heart*', and 'if you confess with your mouth the Lord Jesus and believe in your *heart* that God has raised him from the dead, you will be saved. For with the *heart* one believes to righteousness, and with the mouth confession is made to salvation' (Romans 10:8–10). I have put the word 'heart' in italics to emphasise the importance of making verbal faith confessions out of genuine heart convictions. But it is equally important to understand the connection between genuine heart *conviction*, and the *confession* of faith. You cannot have one without the other.

Confession and conviction

Faith confession is not empty, religious repetition of the Word of God. That amounts to superstition and has nothing to do with the genuine Word of faith. The Word of faith begins in the heart when we receive God's truth for our life, and once that Word generates a firm conviction within our heart, it begins to affect what we say; and more than that, what we do. Confession arises out of conviction. It's not just quoting Scripture: a parrot can quote Scripture. One of our staff workers has a wonderful parrot called 'Cockie' that talks so well I am sure that she could teach it to recite Bible verses! But that's not confession. Many Christians speak the Word of God mechanically and expect him to be impressed. That's absolutely not what faith is all about because such speaking is empty.

Jesus addresses this problem in Matthew 15:8: 'These people draw near to Me with their mouth, and honour Me with their lips, but their heart is far from Me.' Honouring God with our lips is not enough. *It must also be a reflection of what's going on in your heart.* So faith comes first by hearing the Word of the Lord, and then receiving that Word, believing it, deep in our heart. And that's not talking about our emotions. The heart in the Bible is not just about how we feel. The heart in the Bible is how we really are inside, the inner person. And this is where we need to receive the Word of the Lord, not just paying lip service to it with the emotions or intellect alone, but holding it deeply, inwardly and spiritually. In this way we believe God, even if it doesn't feel good to do it or we cannot fully understand it.

So the confession of faith arises out of the conviction of faith. It is agreeing with the Word in this double sense: our mouth is in agreement with our heart which is in agreement with the Word of the Lord. The seed of the Word takes root in our heart and the firstfruits of it is what we say, what we confess with our mouth. That's why confessing the Word has been a vital part of the Christian faith from the beginning. Some scholars claim that in Romans 10 we find the earliest Christian confession that was probably made at baptism. All believers are joined together, united by this one confession: 'Jesus is Lord.'

I have often heard the statement, 'Confession brings possession', and in certain contexts I can readily agree with it. I understand that as we continue to confess by faith the Word of the Lord, the promised manifestation

eventually becomes ours. But when we look closely at
the process of faith, we find that we do not possess
because we confess. Rather, we confess because we
possess. It's the confession of the faith in our heart
that leads ultimately to the fulfilment of God's promise
in our life. To put it another way, we are not saved
because we 'talk saved'. We 'talk saved' because
we are saved! We are not healed because we 'talk
healed'. We are healed by the Word of God through
faith and we talk healed because we have received
the promise in our heart. That's a very important
distinction, because faith is not positive thinking or
mind over matter, as if by saying it enough times it
will become true. Our confession does not make it true.
We confess with words of faith because it is true and
we know it is true because the Word of God declares
that it is true. Because we believe God's Word in a
particular situation, our words naturally line up with
the pronouncements of God's Word concerning it.

I want to go a little further, and to explain how and
why all this is true. It has to do with the way God has
made our human personality to function.

The heart

Proverbs 4:23 says, 'Keep your heart with all diligence,
for out of it spring the issues of life.' Above all, guard
your heart. God doesn't just say, 'Watch what you do',
or 'Watch what you say', but 'Watch what *you are in
your heart*.' We can be convinced that the Christian
faith is true, and even make some kind of commitment
to follow it; but unless we are in a genuine heart
relationship with God it will never work. It remains
only outward confession and outward behaviour, and
is not faith which begins in the heart. We are told to

watch our heart carefully because *out of it* spring the issues of life. Like a fountain, what is in it flows out of it. Everything that we say and do is an overflow of our inner personality, our heart. If our heart is right then right speech and right actions will follow. It is what is in our heart that counts before God.

What comes out of us is an expression of what's within us. That's a spiritual principle, and it is reiterated again in Proverbs 27:19, 'As in water face reflects face, so a man's heart reveals the man.' If we look in the mirror we see the reflection of what we actually look like. We can't deny it, there it is in front of us. As the mirror shows how we look, the heart exposes what we are really like. We may say one thing but believe something else. Our heart is a most accurate barometer of who we really are. There is an amusing reference to this in Proverbs 23:7. Here we have a man, I don't know who he was, possibly a businessman or some dignitary with lots of entertaining to do, but his heart is not in it. He's very stingy and he says to his guests, 'Have some more. Eat up, there's plenty', but inside he's thinking, 'I hope they don't take it!' Now the Bible says of him, 'As he thinks in his heart, so is he. Eat and drink, he says to us, but his heart is not with us.' So what's going on in the heart is a true reflection of the person.

Then in Matthew 12:33–7, Jesus takes this principle one step further. It's the principle of *overflow*. Think what happens to your bath tub. You are running the bath, the telephone rings, you forget that the bath is running and the water goes down the overflow instead of over the edge of the bath. That's why every bath has an overflow; hardly a great theological fact! But every person also has an overflow: it's our mouth. From the abundance, or overflow of the heart, the mouth speaks. What is in the bath is the same as what overflows out of the bath when it gets full. What is in our heart will overflow through our mouth. That's why Jesus says, 'Either make the tree good and its fruit good, or else make the tree bad and its fruit bad; for a tree is known by its fruit . . . A good man out of the good treasure of his heart brings forth good things, and an evil man out of the evil treasure brings forth evil things' (Matthew 12:33, 35).

Faith confession

If our heart is full of faith, it will overflow out of our mouth in confession. Our mouth will be full of faith words because our heart is full of faith. Our speech will reflect the attitude of faith that's in our heart, and this principle of heart confession is so strong that Jesus said we will be judged by every careless word that we speak. He is not talking about literally every word, but every *careless* word. We are not going to be judged only by what we say, because on another occasion Jesus says, 'Therefore by their fruits you will know them. Not everyone who says to me, "Lord, Lord" shall enter the kingdom of heaven, but he who does the will of My Father in heaven' (Matthew 7:20–1).

So he's not talking about being judged by our polished, carefully presented, or deceiving words, he's talking about those careless words that really reflect what's going on in our heart. It's those slip-of-the-tongue statements which we didn't mean to say, but actually reveal what we are thinking in our heart. Those careless words and the overflow of our heart truly reveal what's going on inside us. It's on that same principle that faith operates. If our heart is full of faith, the fruit will be faith fruit, faith words, faith actions. What we say and do will be consistent with our faith, because it will be based on what we believe in our heart. What is in our hearts is seen most clearly during times of testing. When trying circumstances shake us up, what overflows out of our mouth is what is in our heart. That is why Jesus said that if we believe and do not doubt in our heart, it will be done for us (Mark 11:23). We must make sure faith is genuinely a part of our inner life.

All this is so important because it is at the very centre of the Gospel and is what sets it apart from all other beliefs, and all other religions. The Christian faith is not about *doing*, it is about *being*. Being born again, being a child of God. *The doing flows from the being*. That is why Jesus said, 'You must be born again' (John 3:3–7). It is not a matter of changing your outward behaviour, or even simply holding to a new set of beliefs, it is about receiving a totally new life from God and allowing this new life to find expression, in your beliefs, thoughts, motives and your external lifestyle. It's rather like having a well of polluted water inside us, and therefore, no matter how hard we try, whatever we pump out of the well is polluted by what is contained within it. Until the well is totally cleansed, every effort to get pure water is useless. The Bible teaches that the heart is just like a polluted well, and we need to receive a new purified heart from God so that what comes out of it will be pleasing to God.

It is the same principle as a tree and its fruit. A good tree bears good fruit. That's why we need to be born again. Until we believe in Jesus Christ we are a bad tree, or that's the true condition of our heart. Outwardly we may look impressive, appear upright and act like a decent, moral person, but inside we are quite another person. The Bible says the heart is deceitful and desperately wicked (Jeremiah 17:9). God is not impressed with how any of us look outwardly. He's concerned with our need to have that evil nature uprooted from within us and God's nature planted in us. It is called being born again, so that inside us will be a new nature that will begin to bear fruit in our life. That is exactly what God promises to do:

> I will give you a new heart and put a new spirit within you; I will take the heart of stone out of your flesh and give you a heart of flesh. I will put My Spirit within you and cause you to walk in My statutes, and you will keep My judgments and do them. (Ezekiel 36:26, 27)

If you can genuinely accept this and be willing to let God work in you like that, then you can be born again. It is futile to try and live the Christian life without the Christian nature, and only God can give it to you, but you can be sure he will, if you ask him.

All this shows us how pointless it is to turn confession into some kind of faith technique. We can confess for ever a truth with our lips but if the same truth is not held in our heart nothing will come of it. This does not mean that we discount the benefits of Scripture memorisation, or reciting the Bible. In fact, the more we handle the Bible, and become familiar with it, the greater opportunity the Holy Spirit has of causing the Word to touch us, provided of course that we come to the Word in humility, depending on God to reveal it to our heart. *Faith operates from the heart*. And if faith is really there in the heart, then it must be spoken out. That's why without confession, faith cannot operate. The effective working of faith inevitably will lead to us confessing the Word, and that is the real power of faith confession. If we believe and have strong conviction, our confession will line up with the Word of God. Then we have all the power of God's Word operating through our lips. When we speak forth our confession with true faith conviction according to the Word of God, we can cause our circumstances to line up with the promises of God. That's how much power we have when we believe.

Speak to your mountain

Jesus once said to his disciples, 'if you have faith as a mustard seed, you will say to this mountain, "Move from here to there", and it will move; and nothing will be impossible for you' (Matthew 17:20). If there is a mountain of opposition standing in the way, standing between us and the will of God for our life, through faith we have the power and authority to tell that mountain to move, and that mountain will have to obey us. This applies to any circumstance of our life that is outside the will of God for us. The God who said, 'Let there be light!' can bring about all the changes necessary for our circumstances to line up with his will and his Word. The most important aspect of this is that it is not just our choice, or our comfort, but it is God's Word and his glory that is at stake here. Many people think of faith as some kind of bank card with unlimited credit: 'I can have anything I want from God.' In faith, we *can* have everything but, *according to the will of God*, and if God has promised it in his Word, he wants us to have it. And if he wants us to have it, then it is for his glory. It cannot be right to let the mountain or the obstacle that stands in the way of the will, and the glory of God for you, remain. By faith, arising out of a genuine Spirit-filled conviction of the heart, speak to your mountain, and keep on speaking to it, and it *will* be removed!

God wants us to rise in faith above many of our circumstances. I don't believe in open/closed door systems of guidance – if the door is closed, then it is not God's will; if the door is open, it is God's will. I've been through some open doors with disastrous consequences. But now, if God tells me to go in a direction and the door is closed, I kick it down in the name of Jesus! I am not a circumstantial Christian: I don't believe we should be. *Faith is all about challenging your circumstances with the Word of God*. Of course we face facts, but we reckon with faith. Abraham faced the fact that his body was as good as dead and that his wife was barren. He faced the facts, but he reckoned according to faith. He had the promise of God, 'I have made you the father of many nations.' He knew his body was incapable of fulfilling God's promise in a natural sense. Don't run from facts, don't hide from them, don't pretend they aren't real. If we are sick, we are sick. Face the facts. That's why I, for example, counsel people not to stop taking medicine until there is medical confirmation of their healing, especially when not taking that medicine could be dangerous. We have got to be sensible. We live in a world of facts, and physical laws, but these do not have the final say. God's truth has the final say. Faith has the capacity to reach into the unseen realm of those truths and to impose them upon the physical facts of our circumstances around us.

God's implanted life

In this chapter I have highlighted the vital importance of faith speaking the Words of God, Words which first have been received with heartfelt conviction before they rise in powerful intercession, confession, proclamation, declaration and command, so that our world can be shaped according to the will of God. Where are we in our personal world right now? Maybe *we are* the world that needs to be changed. Perhaps you have never personally accepted the new life of Jesus Christ that he offers you. Some of you may be struggling to bring forth good fruit but you are still a bad tree, and that's why it's so difficult for you. Stop trying; it's impossible in your own strength. Give it up and become a good tree! Let him implant his life in you so that your words and your works from now onwards will be motivated by God's Spirit within you.

And the message for Christians – however experienced – is that it's time to line up totally with the Word of God, and we can begin now by getting to know the promises in the Bible, believing them, then *confessing* them. The Word is near you; it is in *your mouth* and in your heart; that is, the Word of faith *you* are proclaiming (Romans 10:8).

7 Doing the Word

Thus also faith by itself, if it does not have works, is dead (James 2:17).

One of the greatest privileges I have in my role as pastor of Kensington Temple is to serve the international vision of the fellowship. It is not hard to be aware of the needs of the nations when there are over one hundred different nationalities represented in your church. This, coupled with a personal call to the nations, has meant that I have gone on frequent short-term missions in many parts of the world. I am always blessed and enriched by these times and they have often proved to be great adventures of faith as well as enormous fun.

God certainly has a sense of humour and it is often seen by the way he deals with us. I remember one very early mission trip to Kenya that I led many years ago. From the beginning, it was one great faith lesson, organised by the Holy Spirit. That's another way of saying it was a series of disasters waiting to happen! We were all very inexperienced in missions work, and although I was born in Kenya, it was my first time back in the country for many years, and things had changed a great deal.

When we arrived at Nairobi airport, we were greeted with the news that there had been a breakdown in organisation, and we were told that we had no transport, no equipment and no itinerary. I wanted to catch the next plane home, but I couldn't. I was the team leader!

And so I pretended to be perfectly in control of the situation and went about picking up various electrical items from the city. We had intended to go into the mountains of the Rift Valley region and show the Campus Crusade film, *Jesus*, based on Luke's gospel. It was available both in Kiswahili and Kikuyu, the local languages.

After a great deal of effort, we finally arrived at Nakuru, our base town that would give us access to the mountains. I had managed to beg, borrow or hire most of the equipment we needed; that is, everything but a generator. And do you think I could find one? We could have bought one, but didn't have enough money. The team was becoming more and more frustrated. How could we operate the equipment without a generator?

So I prayed and, I must confess, it was not a particularly spiritual prayer. More like, 'Why have you got me into this mess, Lord?' I was tired, discouraged and totally unaware I was at school. The Holy Spirit was teaching me something. Pulling myself together I thought to give it one last try. I went down the main street looking for an electrical supplier, and went into the only one I saw.

As I entered the shop, something happened to me. I felt a peculiar excitement, a strange tingling inside. I had intended simply to ask in general terms about hiring a generator. But instead, I found myself walking up to a young Asian man behind the counter, and saying, 'I have come for the generator.' The young man glanced up from his papers on the counter and turned back to his work, 'What generator?' I began to explain that I was going up country to show a Gospel film and I needed a generator. Then I added, 'Free of charge – I have no money.' Without saying anything else, the shop assistant picked up the telephone and made a call. A few minutes later, I was in another shop, tucked away behind the main street. The young man had directed me there, and given me a note to deliver to the owner.

The second man's English was not good, and my Kiswahili was even worse! But after a time we got through to each other. The old man disappeared for ages into the store room. Finally, he came back covered in dust and cobwebs, with a huge grin of satisfaction carrying a generator. He dropped it gently on to the floor in front of me. 'O thank you, Asante! Asante!' I said shaking him by the hand. 'Can I have it free, please – no charge?' I added tentatively. 'Of course. No charge' was his confident reply.

I could not wait to get back to the others to tell them about how God had provided. Of course I made a big thing of it, and helped everyone understand how we were about God's business and he was ready to give us everything we needed for his work. I was now trying to be the teacher, but little did I realise that I was still the student, being firmly tutored by the Holy Spirit. It soon became apparent. No matter how hard we worked, we could not get the generator to work. 'No wonder the man said, "No charge"', someone quipped; 'It is absolutely free of charge!' I chuckle now as I write this, but I can assure you I did not find it humorous then.

I could have kicked myself, or the generator, or both! I had boasted too soon. What were we going to do now? Richard, one of the team, had some engineering skills and he did what work he could, then he came to me and said, 'It's no use, Colin. I can't make it work.' By this time, I had begun to think about the whole situation, the frustrating time we had had ever since we set foot in the country, our purpose in coming, the powerful Gospel film we wanted to show in the language of the people and that we truly believed God had sent us. I stood up with renewed determination. 'Come,' I said, walking towards the rest of the team. I called everyone to gather round, and we looked down at that useless piece of equipment. 'It doesn't make sense', I began. 'God would not provide us with a generator that doesn't work. If he provided it, *he* will make it work!' With that we prayed. Some commanded, others laid hands on the machine and still others walked around it like lions stalking their prey! When we finished we were confident of one thing: we were now in possession of the most blessed piece of equipment in Kenya!

Richard, who by then had earned the nickname *Fundi*, or 'Fix-it man', knelt down beside the generator and gave the cable a tug. Nothing happened. He tried several times again, and then finally he shouted, 'It works!' And with that the confirmation came as the little generator chugged into life! We were ecstatic. That machine served us well from then on. Although it was still extremely temperamental, we had all learned the secret. It worked by prayer! Before we started the film, we gathered around it and prayed. Often we would leave someone near the generator for the whole evening, so that every time it faltered, and the movie projector would slow down, throwing weird, bass sounds out into the African night there would be an instant prayer response to put it right.

And that is how it happened. Many hundreds of people came to Christ through our efforts. Helped by this and many other challenges to our faith that trip our faith grew stronger and we even saw many miracles of healing among the people.

Faith is an exciting adventure, and it is worth persevering. We must now take this teaching on faith further. My experience in Kenya taught me faith requires bold *actions*. If faith has a language, faith also has a lifestyle. Faith has actions. A lifestyle is not just what we say but how we live. It's not just what we *believe*, but what we *do*.

The link between faith and actions (doing the Word) is something James taught as a fundamental part of the Gospel: 'What good is it, my brothers, if a man claims to have faith but has no deeds? Can such faith save him? Suppose a brother or sister is without food or clothes? If one of you says to him, go, I wish you well, keep warm and well fed, but does nothing about his physical needs, what good is it? *Thus also faith by itself, if it does not have works [actions], is dead*' (James 2:17). That's the verse I want to concentrate on because it identifies the *essence* of discipleship.

Verbal and visible results

Living faith is active. It affects the way we talk. What is in our heart will come out of our mouth. But faith has visible as well as verbal results. Genuine faith will be both seen and heard. It will be heard in our words and seen in our actions; after all, what we do shows what we believe. This is the principle of 'by their fruits you will know them'. What's inside us will be made plain by what comes out of us. It's the principle of roots and fruits. The kind of fruit that a tree produces is determined by the kind of tree it is. In the same way our behaviour is determined by who we are and our nature inside. If we are full of faith, our actions will be faith actions. This is how faith operates, and without this operation we have dead faith and empty religion.

It's not just what we say but what we do that truly reveals what's in our heart. If you have belief without action, then you don't have faith. And if you have action without belief, it's not real biblical action. *Faith and obedience are two sides of the same coin.* If we have faith but no obedience it's not faith at all, but *empty words.* If we have obedience without faith it's not true obedience, just *empty works.* To obey God we must believe that he is and that he rewards those who seek him. Without faith, it is impossible to please God. True obedience must be accompanied by inner faith; but on the other hand, it's not enough just to believe: we must also take action. If we say we believe and do nothing about it, then we don't really believe what we say. True faith is always exhibited in action, positive faith actions. And these actions correspond exactly with the operation of faith that is happening internally. Faith is supremely active. It is a belief in action as Hebrews chapter 11 clearly shows.

Faith's roll of honour

Hebrews 11 shows how active faith really is. It gets results, it achieves things, it's so practical and down to earth.

By faith Abel offered a sacrifice. By faith Enoch was taken from this life. By faith Noah built an ark. By faith Abraham left Ur and made his home in the promised land. By faith Abraham was enabled to become a father, even though he was past age and Sarah his wife was barren. By faith he offered Isaac as a sacrifice when God tested him. By faith, Isaac blessed Jacob and Esau. By faith Jacob blessed each of Joseph's sons. By faith Joseph spoke about the Exodus and gave instructions about his bones. It was a truly amazing act of faith that Joseph should speak about the exodus from Egypt and tell them to make sure they took his bones with them. By faith Moses' parents hid him. By faith Moses refused the call of Egypt and left Egypt keeping the passover. By faith the Israelites miraculously passed through the Red Sea. By faith the walls of Jericho fell. By faith Rahab was preserved as she welcomed the spies of Israel. Then there are the other exploits of faith. Kingdoms were conquered, justice was administered, promises of God were fulfilled, lions' mouths were shut, fiery flames were quenched. People escaped death by the sword, weakness was turned to strength, people became powerful in battle. Foreign armies were routed, the dead were raised, tortures were endured, people accepted destitution, persecution and all kinds of mistreatment, and it was *all* by faith.

Faith without actions

If faith is not active then it's dead; it's not really faith at all. At this point I want to clear up a confusion that often exists over the statement in James 2:24: 'You see then that a man is justified by works, and not by faith only.' This even stumbled Martin Luther who was the father of the Reformation, the great Protestant move of God when the Church in the sixteenth century was reawakened and reinvigorated by the Gospel of Jesus Christ. Martin Luther, a young Augustinian monk, felt no peace with God, although he had fulfilled every religious requirement given to him by his spiritual leaders. After a long period of intense personal agony and much study and searching of the Scriptures, he finally understood from the Word of God that a person is justified by faith apart from works. This means that good works, whether religious acts of worship or moral acts of decency, are totally incapable of gaining anyone entrance into the kingdom of God. The apostle Paul explains we are saved by 'God's grace through faith,

not works' (Ephesians 2:8,9). Luther rightly concluded
that we are declared righteous by God, not because of
what we do, but through faith in Jesus Christ. But
unfortunately he was not fond of the book of James
and called it 'the epistle of straw', because he could not
understand James' emphasis on good works. Actually
Paul and James are saying exactly the same thing. You
are not saved by good works, you are saved *for* good
works, but good works done in faith. Ephesians 2:10
follows on from the grace of God that comes through
faith with the statement, 'For we are His workmanship,
created in Christ Jesus for good works, which God prepared beforehand that we should walk in them.' James
also teaches this and says, 'Yes, we are justified by
faith, but if it is real faith *it will be seen* in what we do.'

If we think we can be Christians and live as we
choose, then we haven't understood salvation. True
faith is obedient. It is hearing and *obeying* God's
Word. We cannot truly believe and live independently
of God's truth operating in our life. When we truly
believe, God gives us his power to live a new life.
By turning our life right round through the power of
God, we no longer live for ourselves but for God. That
takes a lifestyle of faith, not just one or two actions of
faith once in a while. We are called to live and to go
on living by faith standing on the Word of God.

So in God's plan, faith and actions work together
as partners complementing each other. Look at James
1:17 which says, 'Thus also faith by itself, if it does
not have works, is dead.' As the body without the spirit
is dead, so faith without action is dead. If it is not
accompanied or partnered by action it is dead and not
real faith at all. Why? Because faith without action is
incomplete. Verse 22, speaking of Abraham says, 'Do
you see that faith was working together with his works,
and by works faith was made perfect?' Abraham's faith

was made complete by what he did. His faith and his actions were working in partnership. Faith and action, in God's economy, go together. You can't have the one without the other.

One young man came to me for prayer. 'I want a job', he said. I was happy to pray for him, but wondered what he was doing practically in order to find work. 'O nothing', he replied nonchalantly, 'I am trusting God to find me one.' 'Well, praise the Lord, Tommy!' I came back at him; 'He just has.' 'Really?' he said looking a bit puzzled. 'Yes', I said, 'beginning 9.00 am Monday morning, your job is to go out and look for employment, in the local shops, parks and the Job Centre.' Of course this did not guarantee that he would actually find work, but at least he was doing something practical, and putting his faith into action.

Like Tommy, our faith is incomplete in so many areas. We have begun to believe and to move forward in faith but we have not yet completed our faith with appropriate action. With every expression of faith there is always a corresponding action of faith that God wants us to perform. In every situation in which God calls us to believe him, there is something he wants us to do in faith. You may say, 'I've done all that I can do. There is nothing more to do but pray.' Well, *that's* an action of faith, particularly if having prayed, you can agree to stop worrying about it! Simply laying something at the feet of Jesus and trusting him for the outcome is a great action of faith! It takes effort not to worry, but faith never worries, it trusts. People should be able to look at our lives and say, 'I don't understand you Christians, you should be worried but you're not!' The fact is we have a God who takes care of us in all situations and circumstances of life.

Shelly had been having a lot of trouble with Roy, her teenage son. Since the death of the boy's father, Shelly had found all the difficulties of single parenthood weighing heavily on her. Roy was getting into the wrong company at school, staying out late at nights and falling behind in his school work. She often cried as she felt the distance increasing between them. But Shelly kept up the home and maintained the steady income for them both. She took advice from the head teacher at school, and found ways of encouraging Roy to make the right friends; she also called on the help of her cousin, an older man whom Roy could relate to. In fact she did everything that she could possibly do to help the situation. Roy was still as rebellious as ever and she felt crushed by her own anxiety. In this situation, there was nothing more for her to do. There were no slick 'faith steps' she could take to change what was happening. Instead, she resolved to leave the situation in God's hands. She had done her part, now all she could do positively was to deal with her own anxiety. Prayer was a great comfort to her and gradually the anxiety subsided. She knew God was in control of her life, and that of her son.

The action that arises out of faith is usually very specific. It is not merely being active, doing something. We are very good at being active. Sometimes we are so busy doing things that true, appropriate faith action has no opportunity to express itself. Evangelical and charismatic Christians are perhaps the supreme activists. We can keep ourselves so busy, we make world leaders look like layabouts! Our activities seem so impressive. But God says, 'I want your works, your actions and your deeds to be *appropriate* to your faith.' It's not just doing but it's doing the right thing, taking appropriate action which *exactly corresponds* with the specific step of faith being taken. For every operation of faith there is a corresponding action that faith demands. For example, if we profess faith in a

God of love, then our actions should reflect that faith. We should love and care for others by what we say and how we behave towards them. Otherwise it shows we really do not believe in the love of God at all. Our faith is seen by what we do. Our actions must correspond to our faith. To help us understand this principle, let us look at three examples from James chapter 2.

Caring for the poor

James demonstrates how important it is to have appropriate works to match the faith that we profess in relation to the poor and needy: 'If a brother or sister is naked and destitute of daily food, and one of you says to them, "Depart in peace, be warmed and filled", but you do not give them the things which are needed for the body, what does it profit?' (James 2:15–16). It is easy to see the appropriate faith action that should be accompanied by that faith pronouncement. What good is it, James asks, if it is only words? If we have it within our means to give to the poor, then words alone are not enough. They are empty, faithless words. But true faith-filled words will be accompanied by faith-directed actions.

Sacrificing a son

In James 2:21–2, he says, 'Was not Abraham our father justified by works when he offered Isaac his son on the altar? Do you see that faith was working together with his works, and by works faith was made perfect?' The word 'perfect' here means complete or mature. Abraham's faith was made complete, brought to maturity, by what he did. His faith was validated by

his actions. Now we have to read this text very carefully
to see the kind of faith pronouncement that Abraham's
action validated. It says in verse 21 that Abraham
offered his son Isaac on the altar. God had told
Abraham that Isaac would be the child of promise and
he knew that the whole plan of God was focused on his
son's life. Abraham was so sure that the promises were
going to be fulfilled, that even if Isaac were sacrificed,
he expected God to step in with his solution. The Bible
shows that Abraham had actually reasoned in his mind
what, if it came to it, God would do. He thought about
it and said, 'Lord, you told me to sacrifice my son,
but my son must live in order for your promises to
be fulfilled, so after I've sacrificed him, you will have
to raise him from the dead.' Abraham's faith travelled
that far and it was accompanied by appropriate actions
all the way. It says in Genesis 22:5 that as Abraham
began to climb the mountain, to the place of sacrifice,
he turned and said to his servants, 'Stay here with the
donkey; the lad and I will go yonder and worship, and
we will come back to you.'

So we can see that Abraham's action of sacrificing
his son spoke of a profound conviction and belief in
the promise of God, and God's power to fulfil it. His
actions were totally consistent with his beliefs and his
faith in God. He said, 'I'm going to do it, Lord, and
then you're going to resurrect him', and Hebrews 11:19
says, figuratively speaking, that he did receive his son
back to life, because Isaac was saved from death in the
split second it took for God to say, 'Abraham! That's
enough, stop!'

On the winning side

Isn't it extraordinary that James should choose Rahab

as an example of faith. She was a Gentile prostitute, not
the mother of the faithful! James 2:25 says, 'Likewise,
was not Rahab the harlot also justified by works when
she received the messengers and sent them out another
way?' Before Joshua took Jericho, he sent spies into
the city just to check it out. The spies were discovered
and just as they were about to be arrested, Rahab the
harlot hid them, waited until everything was calm, and
then sent them off in safety. God says that those actions
were the actions of faith. She was a believing woman,
and what she did was the outworking of her faith and
a sign of her repentance, as she chose a new direction
for her life.

This woman Rahab had enough faith to reason that
the God of the nations was fighting for Israel and, on
the basis of that, she understood that God had given
them not just Jericho, but the whole land! What great
faith! I wish that kind of faith was alive in the Church
today! If Rahab believed, why can't we believe that
God will give us the victories we need today. We must
begin to lay hold of the great possibilities of God for
our generation. If every Christian was prepared to reach
out to one other person we would double the impact in
our nations. If every Christian took up one practical act
of service in their town or community, our lights would
shine across the world. However God calls us to do it,
whether as part of a large, growing church, small house
group fellowships or as individual believers making a
difference where we are, we must start putting our faith
into action.

Rahab said, 'I know that the Lord has given this land
to you, so I'm going to hide you and protect you. And
when I've done that, remember me. I want to be on the
winning side.' That was her faith pronouncement and
its corresponding faith action, working together with
her faith. She didn't just say 'I know God has given

you the land.' She *really* believed it and was prepared to do something about it.

If we really believe that Jesus Christ is Lord, we will do something about it. If we really believe that he wants to reach the lost, we are going to be prepared to do something about it. It's not enough just to say we believe and to sit back passively. It is time to rise up with the mighty works of faith and to do the kind of exploits God calls us to do in our own nation and across the world.

8 Faith's Tests

My brethren, count it all joy when you fall into various trials, knowing that the testing of your faith produces patience. But let patience have its perfect work, that you may be perfect and complete, lacking nothing (James 1:2–4).

Holding on to the promises and the goodness of God during times of suffering is the greatest challenge to faith. And yet this is the very thing that brings our faith to maturity and closer to its object, Jesus Christ. I have found this out in times of intense personal pain. Our second daughter, Laura suffered severe brain damage after birth due to an infection. The devastation and hurt this caused my wife and me are hard to describe. Despite the many improvements we have seen that are nothing short of miracles in Laura's life, she still is totally dependent and virtually unable to do anything for herself. Our faith is passing through the fiery furnace, but we know God is the divine forger and he is working his purpose through it all. Outside the Word of God, this is perhaps the single greatest cause of the growth of faith in my life.

Exercising faith is a process. Each successive phase is like interlocking links in a chain. If that chain is broken the whole process of faith is held back, faith is impaired, and it can easily cease to function altogether. In the last few chapters we have been looking at the vital links in the chain of faith. We can now understand that faith begins with hearing and believing the Word and that the process continues with confessing and doing the Word. Now we come to the next link, *standing firm on the Word*. This is necessary because, if faith is to be fully developed and reach maturity, it must be tested. No one would travel on a plane, knowing that it had never been tested for safety. In the same way faith must first pass the tests.

The testing of faith

Without tests faith cannot come to fruition. Trials and testing are absolutely essential for the development of faith. It can only come to maturity and receive its reward after it has first been tested. But the trouble is that when we get to this point, most of us are horrified, and we give in to pressure saying, 'I thought it was supposed to be easy, but my situation has got worse and worse.' I have heard many people say things like this, 'The moment I tried to believe, it got worse.' Or, 'I determined to trust God for my finances, but my bank balance went to zero.' And, 'When I tried to trust God for my health, I got as sick as a dog.' Or, 'I went out and out for victory but now I'm more defeated than ever.'

We are experiencing *faith's tests*. If we want our faith to triumph it must first be tested. Faith that is not tested cannot triumph, but *faith tested is faith triumphant*. Many people want the triumph without the tests. They want the degree without the examination. There are no short cuts with God: first the examination, then the qualification. Smith Wigglesworth used to say that great triumphs come out of great tests. This great man of faith knew what it was to take his stand on the Word of God and there he would remain, come life or death, until God fulfilled his Word. He went through several years of physical agony, believing God alone would heal him of a kidney condition. Finally, the suffering ended, and God stepped in. Wigglesworth emerged from the experience stronger than ever and continued to bring healing and salvation to thousands.

If we want faith like that, we have to know how to handle tests and how to endure trials. Otherwise after the first hurdle we will say, 'It doesn't work!' Once when I was encouraging a church member to believe God in a difficult situation, she replied, 'I tried that, pastor, and it doesn't work.' 'What have you tried?' I asked. 'I've tried *that* Scripture and it doesn't work!' Apologising I said, 'I'm very sorry, God must have got it wrong there! Give me your Bible, let me take that bit out!' She began to understand what I meant and later went on to have a great victory in her life. We are not called to live our lives along the line of least resistance or to take the easiest path.

We have to go God's way, and as we push forward there will be many mountains of opposition in our way, and many valleys of testing and trial. But the wonderful thing is that every testing and trial of our faith actually develops our faith and enables it to function! Tests mature us. Jesus always dealt with people in this way in order to develop their faith. And he's not changed a bit! Think of the occasion when Jesus' friend Lazarus was sick. He waited a couple more days *knowing* that Lazarus would die. That was a test. How about the Syro-Phoenician woman who came crying to Jesus for help? He said to his disciples, 'Tell her that I'm not going to give the bread that is meant for the children to dogs.' What is that if it's not a test of faith? That test matured her faith and provoked her to say, 'If you're not going to give me the bread that is due to the children, then give me the crumbs that fall from their table – even the dogs get them! I want my little girl to be healed!' She got what she asked for because of her faith; under trial, her faith proved to be genuine. The same was true for the woman who had suffered from internal bleeding for twelve years. She had to fight through the crowd and every step of the way, for this sick woman weakened by the loss of blood, must have been like climbing Mount Everest. But as she continued to push forward, her faith was being developed and matured. Finally, she touched the hem of Jesus' garment and was gloriously healed.

Think of Peter's words in 1 Peter 1:6–7. Having spoken of our incorruptible inheritance waiting for us in heaven, Peter goes on to say, 'In this you greatly rejoice, though now for a little while, if need be, you have been grieved by various trials, that the genuineness of your faith, being much more precious than gold that perishes, though it is tested by fire, may be found to praise, honour, and glory at the revelation of Jesus Christ.' Our portion is not just the inheritance but also the trials that develop the faith necessary to receive the inheritance. The Word of God tells us in advance to expect all kinds of trials, so that our faith might pass through the fire and be proved genuine.

Many people expect an easy ride as a Christian. But the more we want to grow in faith, the more God will allow the devil to send trials our way. 'Why did God let this happen?' we ask. The answer may not be comfortable, but it's glorious. Our faith is more precious than gold, but even gold has to be tried, it has to be purified in the furnace. If that's what we do with the precious metal gold, why are we surprised that God wants to allow us to go through the furnace-like affliction of the trials and testings so that when the heat is on, our faith may emerge as pure gold? If our faith won't stand the test of trials, it's not genuine faith. It's a 'Please-me-thank-you-Jesus' mentality.

No quick fix

So God's tests are necessary to mature faith, to purify it and demonstrate its genuineness, because God will only reward genuine faith. He won't reward a selfish, immature or demanding mentality. Just imagine Job singing one of our modern choruses, 'Blessed be the name of the Lord, blessed be the name of the Lord, most high . . .' 'What are you singing about Job?' 'Well, I've lost my farm, I've lost my riches, I've lost my family, but the Lord has given and the Lord has taken away, so, "Blessed be the name of the Lord . . ."' *The time to sing, is when you are under trial.* Don't pretend everything is all right when it is not, but praise him in all things. Job wasn't rejoicing because everything was all right or because he wasn't feeling the pain of his situation. He was rejoicing because he discerned the goodness of God in it all. He said, 'I will not just serve God for what I can get out of him, I will serve God because I love him.' This is the only true basis for service. We can often trace the development of our faith in the midst of the trial, and be thankful for what God is teaching us through what is happening. That's true faith.

Developing character

Our faith pleases God when we say, 'I don't understand why you haven't given this to me now, but you know best and I'm trusting you.' We love God for himself and faith that allows us to keep on loving

God despite our circumstances pleases him. Faith works by love, and love must also work by faith. These tests are absolutely necessary to develop a character strengthened by love. God is looking for mature sons who are in his likeness, who share his character. There's nothing more harmful than giving unconditionally to immaturity. God loves us too much to do that. In blessing us, God wants us also to grow in maturity.

That is why James encourages us to rejoice in times of trial. Trials, handled correctly, bring maturity. 'My brethren, count it all joy when you fall into various trials, knowing that the testing of your faith produces patience. But let patience have its perfect work, that you may be perfect and complete, lacking nothing' (James 1:2–4). If we are mature, God can trust us with everything. That's why we will not lack anything. But the key is standing up under trial. That above all, develops patience and character. People who have these qualities will not easily abuse God's gifts. They will not put his gifts before his Person. We must learn to seek the face of God and not just his hand.

In the early days when I began to minister abroad my children were quite young, and I would come back from Africa and always have some gifts for the family. Sometimes I thought they were more pleased to see what I was bringing than to see me! 'Hello Daddy, you're back! What have you got for us?' But now, what I bring back – well they're very interested but they say, 'Thank you, that's nice. Now how are *you*? Tell us about the trip.' That's a little more mature isn't it? In the same way, when we learn to focus on God, on his Person and his love, and seek to please him, our motives become pure and our character becomes developed. Then God can trust us with his gifts. He can trust us with his provision, because he knows that we're not going to mess it all up through immaturity. So tests are absolutely necessary to mature both us and our faith.

How do tests come?

Trials are directed at our faith, to test it. This means our ability to stand firm on the Word of God in a situation where God's Word does not appear to be effective. Therefore tests are directed at the Word and persevering means holding on to the Word no matter what the circumstances. In what ways, then, should we expect trials to come? Tests come in two main ways, through *delays* and *contradictions*.

Delays
In Habakkuk 2:3 God says, 'For the vision is yet for an appointed time; but at the end it will speak, and it will not lie. Though it tarries, wait for it; because it will surely come, it will not tarry.' God often delays his answers to test our faith. At times I think it looks like this:

Heaven: Our answer is all wrapped up and neatly parcelled, stamped and addressed, and the angel is there at the post box, but God says, 'Just wait a bit, hold on for a couple of days and we'll see what's going on down there.'

The earth: 'Lord, I have asked, and I believe I have received, but why hasn't it shown up?'

Heaven: 'Hold on! He's not quite ready to receive.'

Can you see the picture? While we're petulantly stamping our feet on the earth, we're preventing the angel from posting that answer. But when we learn to say, 'Thank you, Jesus, let it come in your timing, because your timing is best', and through faith we release it to the Lord, he says to the angel, 'OK you can post it now.' But most of us give up too soon. Just as we get to the point when the angel is about to post that encouraging answer, we doubt the Word of God and say, 'It can't be the will of God', and God says to the angel, 'Come back. Faith is not ready.' I wonder how many undelivered parcels are waiting up there because we were not at home patiently waiting for the delivery? We have to be ready and prepared so that when God sends his answers, we are in the place where we need to be to receive them.

Hebrews 10:35–7 says, 'Therefore do not cast away your confidence, which has great reward. For you have need of endurance, so that after you have done the will of God, you may receive the promise: For yet a little while, And He who is coming will come and will not tarry.' The context is the second coming of Christ, but every provision which comes in answer to faith comes the same way, and if God has delayed a provision and delayed an answer, don't throw away your confidence. It may well be that God is testing our faith. At that time we must say, 'Lord, I accept this test as a test from you. I am not going to give up believing. I'm going to hold on to my confidence.' After all, the delays of God are only apparent delays. He is never late with his promises. He will keep them and do so always right on schedule.

Fresh out of Bible college, Bill wanted so much to share with others the message of the Gospel. He was soon to do some low-paid social work, to gain experience before entering into the ministry. He put together an evangelistic booklet carrying a few written testimonies from his fellow students who told him how they came to faith in Christ. The local vicar's wife ran a small printing business and she helped him print 500 copies at a cost of £300. 'Pay me when you can', she

said, and although Bill had the firm conviction that
the money would come, months went by, and nothing
happened. The booklet was a great tool for Bill as he
shared his faith with others, but he was concerned
because the amount had to be paid, and he still had
no money.

Bill held on to his conviction, sure it was from the
Lord: 'God will do it.' Finally he wrote a cheque for
the full amount, and posted it. He knew that he could
borrow the amount to meet the payment of the cheque
if necessary, but he was confident that he would not
have to draw on this facility. Sure enough, when he
came back from the post box, a letter was waiting for
him. It was a cheque for over three times the amount
he owed! It was a totally unexpected payment from
his late father's estate. God's timing is perfect!

Contradictions

Contradictions come in three ways: through Satan,
through circumstances, and through people. Satan will
come along and say, 'Did God really promise you
that? Is it really God's will to provide for your every
need? What about those starving millions overseas?
They don't get provided for, so what makes you
think you are any better than them? What about all
those people who are not healed? What makes you so
different from them?' The words may come through
scores of different situations and circumstances but
the serpent's hiss is unmistakable: 'Has God said?'
Suddenly we're thrown into a crisis of confidence, or
personal uncertainty or theological confusion; and yet
all the while God is testing our faith in his Word.

Satan is still attacking God's Word in the way he
did at the beginning. Look at his tactics. 'Has God
indeed said, "You shall not eat of every tree of the
garden"?' (Genesis 3:1). There *was* a restriction, but

God said they could eat of all the fruit except for *one* tree. But the serpent's lie was that God was still deliberately withholding something good from the man and woman. I've noticed that people fail to understand the goodness of God. It seems we have believed the lie that God isn't interested in us. We've been taught that we shouldn't trouble God, that we should look after ourselves and grin and bear our troubles. The British speak about keeping a 'stiff upper lip', but God is not like that. He is not an English gentleman. He does not conform to our social and cultural patterns or norms.

God is a good God and he has good gifts for us. It's God's will to bless us. He wants us to rise up out of our negativity and understand that God is *for* us. Trouble, sickness, hurt and sorrow do not come from him. God is light and in him is no darkness at all. When he made us, he didn't make us sick or create circumstances of evil or trouble. He looked at his creation and was satisfied, 'Then God saw everything that He had made, and indeed it was very good' (Genesis 1:31). God is not evil, Satan is the troublemaker. Of course, God is sovereign and all-powerful and he can even use Satan's tricks to his own advantage. He *will use* trials, and at time sickness, but God doesn't cause these things. Nothing evil has its source in God's nature. He only allows what he can use for our good, and for his glory. God never intended for there to be suffering in the world, but once sin entered it, suffering became a part of life. Now God allows suffering to come to us only to achieve greater purposes than we can sometimes understand or explain. God is a good God, he has good gifts for his children. Don't let the tempter cause you to doubt that. God wants to bless us, and when Satan questions, 'Has God said?', we thunder back, 'Yes! It is written!' (Matthew 4:7).

Peter suffered from a profound sense of rejection

inside. A bright and capable student, he had nevertheless found it hard to make his way in the work place.
He would progress so far and then his surroundings
seemed to close in on him until he could not go on.
He suffered a severe breakdown. He began to read
his Bible for comfort and discovered some wonderful
passages which describe who we are in the eyes of
Christ. Everything about his life seemed to shout
out in contradiction to what he was reading, 'No!
That doesn't apply to you, you're worthless!' It was
extremely difficult at first, but he determined to see
himself the way God's Word described him. Every
day, with the help of a Christian counsellor, he spent a
few minutes meditating on the Scriptures and repeating
them aloud and personalising them. 'I am loved with
an everlasting love' (Jeremiah 31:3); 'I am accepted in
God's beloved son' (Ephesians 1:6). Soon his outlook
changed and he grew in confidence. His life was being
changed by the Word of God.

Faith faces facts

But what do we do with the negative circumstances of
our lives? Our circumstances frequently contradict the
Word of God. If you're going to live in the realm of
circumstances, forget it, you'll never move in faith. If
the circumstances contradict the Word of God to you,
then so much the worse for your circumstances! Faith is
that capacity to step back from your circumstances and
say, 'I face these facts, but I know the truth of the Word,
and I am holding to that. I am not moved by what I can
see, hear, taste, touch or smell.' Faith does not ignore
the facts of a situation. They are real, but they are not
the end of the story. Abraham acknowledged that his
body was as good as dead, and that his wife was barren.

Those were the facts, but the truth was that God had said, 'I have made you the father of many nations', and ultimately it was that truth that Abraham imposed by faith upon every physical fact, until they were all changed and in line with the will of God.

There is a big difference between facts and truth. For example, the fact is that Jesus died as a common criminal condemned under Pontius Pilate. But the truth is deeper than that. He never sinned. The truth is he was God manifest in the flesh. The truth is that as he hung on the cross he was the sacrifice for the sins of the whole world. It is this truth that affects the destiny of nations, and not the external facts of the situation. Facts, as important as they may be, are not as deep as truth. Truth supersedes facts and we must learn to take the truths of the Word of God and superimpose them on the facts of our life. While we face the facts, we can see those very facts transformed when they contradict God's Word. God is *El Shaddai*, the God who transforms us and our circumstances so that they both line up with the revealed will of God, as he did for Abraham (see Genesis 17). When our circumstances contradict the Word of God, something's got to give. And it must be circumstances, because God's Word stands eternal in the heavens. Together with his name and his Word, God is exalted above all things.

In the miracle of the feeding of the crowd, the disciples said, 'Lord, look how hungry these people are. Send them away, because they're going to faint if we don't let them go to get something to eat.' Jesus replied, 'They don't need to go away. You give them something to eat!' Jesus was speaking the truth. The facts were that the disciples only had five loaves and two small fish. But Jesus had spoken, 'You give them something to eat.' The facts of the situation contradicted his Word. How could so little feed so many? It was impossible. But the disciples took Jesus at his Word and despite the facts, did the impossible. Five thousand men together with thousands of women and children were fed from five loaves and two small fish. The impossible became possible, by faith.

Dominated by circumstances?

Are we just going to live in the realm of the possible and only do what other people have done? Are we going to stay imprisoned or limited by the physical facts around us, being dominated by our circumstances that scream out to us in contradiction to the Word of God? Or are we going to believe the Word and watch the facts come into line?

There is no way the Church in the West can take the next step forward until we are a believing people. I'm not just talking about one or two outstanding people who believe, but the whole Christian community. God is not telling us to go where we have not gone before, and through faith to do what we have never done before. Are we going to rise to that challenge? We can begin with those circumstances of our own life that do not line up with the Word of God. We can hold on to the Word of God in the midst of the testing of our faith and come through triumphant and victorious, strong in faith.

So, Satan and our circumstances can often bring direct challenges to the truth of God's Word to us, testing our faith. But I have found that people are often the worst offenders. We have to learn to wear earplugs when we're around certain individuals! The devil will put a few negative people around us to cause us to be shaken in our confidence. Sometimes it's those closest to us whom the devil uses. I'm not suggesting we should alienate ourselves from our friends or from good advice, but whenever people contradict the Word of God, and we are tempted to doubt, we must resist what they say. Jesus turned to Peter, who was questioning Christ's sufferings and death on the cross, and said to him, 'Get behind Me, Satan! Peter, you are not thinking the way God thinks' (Matthew 16:23). Job's wife said to him, 'Curse God and die.' But he said, 'No, I will not. You're not speaking the mind of God. God has given, God has taken away and I'm going to bless him.'

In the middle of the trial it is important to see the objective of the enemy. He wants us to doubt God's goodness and to deny God's Word. But God's purpose in it all is to test our faith and see if we will stand on the Word and remain true to what he has said. That was God's purpose for Israel during the wilderness years, before they entered the promised land (see Deuteronomy 8:2–5). The Lord humbled them and tested them to see what was in their heart, whether they would obey his Word. God allowed them to hunger, and then fed them with manna from heaven. There was no water for them in the desert, but God provided for them. There were no tailors or cobblers but God preserved their clothes and their shoes. And all this in a time of testing! When our faith has been tested, and has been brought to strength and maturity – then we're ready to receive the fulfilment of the promise.

Emotional pain is sometimes the hardest to bear, and Lucy knew it. She was an elderly spinster who had spent some of the best years of her life caring for an invalid mother. Now she was completely alone. There was no one to care for and even her need to be needed was being denied. The loneliness, a sense of loss and her bereavement drove her more and more in on herself, until she felt she could not go on. Out of sheer desperation she told the Lord exactly how she felt. She did not expect the answer that seemed to come immediately from the Holy Spirit: 'No, I don't want you to go on either – not like you are now.' She waited and listened to what she felt God was saying to her: 'I have a work for you to do for me.'

Lucy opened up to the Lord in a new way and from that moment things seemed to change. She also opened up her home, too big for one person, to the weekly youth fellowship. The young people were drawn to caring Lucy and soon they were pouring out their troubles. She felt years younger, even outstripping the youngsters by her indomitable exuberance. After a while her life was so full, she had to pray and ask God to ease up, as she needed a rest!

Lucy came through her test with flying colours, but it was not easy. She had to believe that God was in her circumstances and that he was able to use them as a blessing to her and to others. Faith catches the traces of sun behind the clouds, refusing to deny God's love or to doubt his goodness. That leads us on to the next vital link in the chain of faith – praise.

9 Rejoicing in the Word

Rejoice in the Lord always. Again I will say, rejoice! (Philippians 4:4).

Praise is the authentic language of faith. If we have a genuine attitude of faith, we will be full of praise. Praise reflects the positive, buoyant attitude of a life of faith that honours God no matter what the circumstances. This kind of faith can even praise God for the circumstances which are disastrous according to our normal human understanding, because we realise that those are the very things that strengthen us so that we will be blessed and that God can be glorified. I'm not suggesting that we have a trite little formula here, that if we suffer a tragedy or a terrible accident happens we have to walk around with a smile on our face as if everything is OK. But we praise in faith from the realistic appraisal that God never lets anything come into our life other than what he can use for his glory and for our good.

Rejoicing comes out of a deep, residual and unshakeable belief, a rock-like conviction that God is in control and that we can praise him no matter what the circumstances. It may be raining today but God's glory is shining. Problems may come tomorrow but God stays the same. The Bible teaches that God is 'enthroned upon the praises of his people' (Psalm 22:3), and that when we praise him we acknowledge him for who he is; his eternal unchanging kingdom comes right down to earth and is established amongst us. Praise carries the authority of God, the very authority and power that is needed for us to see the fulfilment of our faith venture. Without it we severely hinder God.

We know that faith is the evidence of things not seen. But some people say, 'When I see it, then I will sing about it, but until then, what is there to sing about?' But God gives us songs in the night time. Paul and Silas were being kept in the inner confines of the maximum security part of the prison; there they began to praise God and magnify him. Songs came in the night and their praises so blessed God that he sent an earthquake just to celebrate! That earthquake shook away their chains (Acts 16). It's a spiritual key. When we don't feel like praising, that's when it is more important than ever to do it. But isn't that hypocritical, to sing when you feel miserable? No, because living by faith is not being led by our feelings. If we're going to live by faith, most of the time we've got to lay our feelings to one side, until they line up with God's Word. If God's Word was altered every time our mood changed, we'd have a 'mood altered' Bible! Today it will tell me, 'Colin you are saved', on Monday mornings it will say, 'No, you're not!' But we're not dependent on our feelings and we do not let them dictate to us. Sometimes following God brings us pain and discomfort. Denying the feelings of the flesh is painful. So in the darkest moment, in the depths of despair, even if it hurts, begin to sing your praise to the Lord, and who knows what earthquake God will send to free you from the chains of your circumstances! Praise can sometimes be a sacrifice that we offer to God, but in the end it brings joy.

Praise brings the victory

There are some special promises in the Word of God for those who learn to praise him in *all* circumstances. Begin by remembering to praise God for who he is. His nature is constant and unchanging, always good, always gracious and always at the peak of his capacity and willingness to bless us. Therefore he is always to be praised, and it lifts your perspective too. As we lift our eyes off our circumstances and on to the beauty and majesty of the Lord Jesus, things don't look so bad. Our praise can also focus our faith on what God is going to do. We can thank him in advance, knowing that he will never leave us or let us down. We can praise him before we see him working. We're going to praise him when he acts so why not praise him before he does it? That's faith!

As I pointed out in the first chapter, faith is the substance of things *not seen*. It is the ability to take hold of some spiritual truth or reality before you see it, or it becomes apparent to the other physical senses. We cannot see Jesus physically, we cannot touch him or in any way appropriate him through our five senses. But nevertheless we love him and we rejoice in him. The Apostle Peter says, 'whom having not seen you love. Though now you do not see Him, yet believing, you rejoice with joy inexpressible and full of glory, receiving the end of your faith – the salvation of your souls' (1 Peter 1:8–9). *Now* is the time to praise him. Some are waiting until they get to heaven before they really start praising the Lord. Don't do that. Start now to develop a lifestyle of praise. It is perhaps even more precious to him to hear us praise him by faith now, than it will be later when we have the benefit of sight. In that day we will be able to look back on our life on the earth and see how the kind hand of God was in all the circumstances of life. But imagine how wonderful it is to praise God before we have this hindsight. Faith gives us that very capacity. We can praise God knowing that he has it all under control. The promise is ours, the manifestation will come, according to the Word of the Lord. If we are living by faith, we will be praising God for what we cannot see as much for what we can see, and maybe even more so!

Those are some good reasons for praising God in all situations, but here's another one. Praise prepares the way for God to bless. The Psalmist says, 'He who sacrifices thank-offerings honours me, and he prepares the way so that I may show him the salvation of God' (Psalm 50:23 NIV). It is good to glorify God in your praise, because it prepares the way for God to act. Honouring God in praise and godly conduct opens the way for the salvation of God, for his deliverance in our situation. Praise is as powerful as that. The clear, logical implication of this verse is that if we fail to praise him with our mouths and our lives, we fail to prepare the way for God to come and bless us. I wonder how many blessings are in the heavenly post box, waiting for us first to learn to praise God. Praise prepares the way for God to come and show us his salvation, whatever the form of salvation we need. If it is a physical healing or any other need, praise will prepare the way for God to come and bless us. I know this is going right against our human inclination, because when we're feeling physically low, praising God is the last thing on our agenda. But thank God we have the Holy Spirit who can help us. Whoever said faith is natural and ordinary? Faith is extraordinary. It is supernatural, empowering us to handle opposition from within ourselves and even from the enemy without.

The Christian life would be simple if we didn't

have this enemy. But we do have a vengeful spiritual opponent, who makes every attempt to break our chain of faith. His tactics are vicious. He will heap on us abuse, fear and intimidation and we must know how to silence him. His words are dangerous as he tries to stumble us in our walk of faith. He tells us that we are stupid to believe God; after all, where is the evidence? He pours scorn on our tottering and feeble steps of faith. He mocks our stumblings and intimidates us with the fear of falling flat on our face, making utter fools of ourselves. He is the arch avenger and when we are successful in destroying his work in one area, he comes back at us spitting and spiteful with the intention of scaring us into never doing it again. If we listen to him we become dwarfs in God, with our faith trimmed like miniature bonsai trees. There is only one answer: silence him! And praise is the way to do it, 'From the lips of children and infants you have ordained praise because of your enemies, to silence the foe and the avenger' (Psalm 8:2 NIV). Simple, childlike faith will always release childlike praises. And these utterances of faith, these songs of joy under pressure and trial, have the power to silence his loudest threats and quench his fiery darts aimed at our spiritual vitality.

The devil cannot stand against the praises of God's children. And this is where we can even begin to go on the offensive. Psalm 149:6–9 takes us further into this truth: 'Let the high praises of God be in their mouth, and a two-edged sword in their hand, to execute vengeance on the nations, and punishments on the peoples; to bind their kings with chains, and their nobles with fetters of iron; to execute on them the written judgment – this honour have all His saints. Praise the LORD!'

Go on the attack

Psalm 8 is all about the defence praise offers. The enemy is on the attack, and we, through our praise, silence him and foil his efforts. But Psalm 149 indicates that praise is also an offensive weapon to be used against the devil. We should not sit and wait for him to come and take vengeance on us; he has done enough harm already. It is time we took our authority to go out and bring vengeance upon him! By faith we must take the offensive against the spiritual forces of evil that assail our lives, attack our loved ones and wreak havoc in society at large. The devil is a liar, a thief and a destroyer, and it's time we got up and made him pay for it! He is a usurper, a terroriser and he acts illegally. That means we have a case against him. Jesus has disarmed him, he is defeated and even destroyed. He is judged already. All we have to do is to execute that judgment against him. It is written in the Word, 'He who is in you is greater than he who is in the world' (1 John 4:4), and we can rise up in the power and victory of our faith and deal with the enemy. Once again praise is the key.

The high praises of God together with the two-edged sword of the Word are enough to bind the evil spiritual authorities and to execute God's judgment written against them. Our praise must be Word-filled praise, and has to do with the promises of faith. As we hold on to our confidence regarding the Word and grow strong in faith, we can give God glory, no matter how fierce the opposition from Satan in our lives. Ultimately we can defeat his every attack and turn it right round so that the very thing that he used to hurt us actually destroys him. This is the glory of *all* God's people, the Psalmist says (Psalm 149:9).

We may have suffered some defeats, but we can

stand up again, and get back into the fight. We are more than conquerors through him. Praise can change a worrier into a *warrior*! Stop taking it lying down. Rise up, with the praise of God in your mouth and the double-edged sword in your hand. Sing to the Lord, take his Word and turn it into powerful declarations of praise and put the enemy to flight. The feeblest saint, through Bible-believing praise, can stand against the strongest demons. God is a good God, the devil's a bad devil! Resist him, oppose him, and defeat him with your praise.

Faith inevitably leads to praise. The Bible says, 'they believed His words; They sang His praise' (Psalm 106:12). The context is a celebration of what God did for the children of Israel when they escaped out of Egypt, and were delivered through the Red Sea. Their deliverance meant the destruction of the enemy. The enemy opposes our victory because our victory is his defeat. When we are moving in praise, we are moving in victory. The waters covered their adversaries, and not one of them survived. That was God's judgments against the enemy. The same is true today, if they refuse to repent and continue to rebel against him.

When Amanda and I were first married, I had just begun my time at Kensington Temple as a junior minister. Amanda was working as a nursing sister, and her salary together with my modest income qualified us for a mortgage on a little flat not far from the church. But we were £5,000 short. Nevertheless we felt inclined to carry on with the purchase believing we were in the will of God. Slightly cheaper accommodation would have taken us much further from the church building than we wanted to be.

I remember the evening clearly in my mind. We sat down at the kitchen table, joined hands in agreement and got set for a long 'battle in the Spirit'. It was as if we were gearing ourselves up to run the London Marathon! But as soon as we uttered the first words of simple petitionary prayer, the answer came, 'Yes.' It was as if someone had taken the wind out of my sails, or like being turned back at Heathrow Airport because the journey was no longer necessary. For a moment I felt a little deflated. I thought this answer was going to take a lot more effort in prayer. With my head still bowed in prayer, I opened one eye and glanced at Amanda. She was beaming. 'Did you hear that?' I asked. 'Yes, I did. He said, "Yes."' We began to laugh. We had both been given an identical inner witness by the Spirit that God had heard our prayer. We did not pray about the matter again; it just wasn't appropriate to do so. All we could do was to praise God, thank him for the answer and look for it to come. Within one week, God had provided every penny!

In every situation, we are called by praise to forge this link in the chain of faith. And if we continue to praise him in faith, believing the promises while carrying the assurance of God's faithfulness to his every Word, we will see the chain of faith complete and we will have the victory. But there is still one more link to make the chain complete, and I shall deal with this in the next chapter.

10 Persevering in the Word

Let us run with endurance the race that is set before us (Hebrews 12:1).

I have been likening faith to a chain of seven interlocking links. Faith is a process involving hearing and believing the Word of God, confessing and doing the Word, enduring tests and praising because of the Word. Before I come to the seventh and final link, I want to point out that if any one of them is weak then the whole chain is in danger. If any one of these links actually breaks then the whole chain of faith will collapse and the faith process itself will be aborted. The life of faith is like running a marathon, not a hundred-yard sprint, and we must keep on running until we cross the finish line. Hebrews 12:1 says, 'let us run with endurance the race that is set before us' and so the seventh and final link is persisting in faith.

The need to persevere

We only inherit the promises through endurance or persistence. God rewards those who *earnestly* seek him (Hebrews 11:6). What is called for is a persistent seeking, a keeping on until the very end with a relentless determination and ongoing diligence. This persistence is absolutely vital. Even in the natural realm if we don't persist at something, we are not going to achieve anything significant. It's that simple. There are very few things worth achieving that we can achieve instantly at the first attempt. We have to persist, and to keep on trying, and sometimes it may take a lifetime. It took Abraham twenty-five years before the promise of a child was fulfilled. It took William Wilberforce and others who worked with him a lifetime of prayer and campaigning before slavery was abolished.

Satan persists; why can't we?

That is why Christians must not give in. We must persist in asserting our faith over our circumstances. Most of us understand that we have powerful spiritual weapons and authority to use them in the name of Jesus Christ. Greater is he that is in us than he that is in the world (1 John 4:4). We know that the devil is insignificant by comparison to God. So why does he have so much influence in the world? One reason is his persistence. He doesn't have many things but one thing he does have is determination. Because he is totally opposed to God he persists until *we* give in. We must reverse that process by being totally obedient to God, persisting in our life of faith until the devil submits to the name of Jesus Christ.

The Greek word used for endurance comes from the idea of remaining behind. I wondered what persistence had to do with remaining behind, but then I remembered the TV advert for one brand of long-lasting batteries which keep on going long after all the others have stopped. That's the life of faith. When everyone else is giving up, we persist. We don't give up, we don't quit. Whatever else we may do – we may slip or slide, we may stumble and fall – but we must never quit, never give in. Persistence is the final link in the chain of faith and if we don't hold on to it the whole chain collapses.

Think of the victory at Jericho (Joshua 6). How many times did they have to walk around that wall? For six days God told them to march around it once each day; and on the seventh day, seven times! Imagine what would have happened on the sixth day if they had given up because they had blisters. Or even if on the final day, they stopped after six times round, and said, 'This is it Joshua, we're fed up. We are going to elect a new leader, one that has mercy on our feet!' If they turned back at that point, would the walls have come down? No. God was testing their faith, finding out what they were made of. He was examining their persistence to find out if they really meant business. But they were obedient to the Lord, they went round each day for six days, and seven times on the seventh day, and then they shouted and the walls came down!

Faith rides the storm

A friend of mine was pastoring a small pioneering work in the Midlands. The little church was in desperate need of new life from outside. They had done all they could think of in order to reach the community for Christ: a youth club had been set up, luncheon clubs for the elderly, and the members had visited all the homes in the locality seeking to make contacts. They were tired and discouraged. There had also been a tragic case of immorality among the leadership in one of the local churches, and it seemed that there was no way of penetrating the hostile barriers people were putting up.

But my pastor friend would not give up. He took them out once more to meet the local people. The members almost refused to go with him. They had actually visited these particular houses and flats five times in the past eighteen months to invite the residents to specific church programmes or for special occasions such as Christmas or Easter. But he insisted, 'Come out one more time with me.' And the breakthrough came. One or two families responded positively which over a period of time led to others coming into the church. The church began to grow rapidly from that time on. The final round made all the difference.

Many people, like Israel at Jericho, are at the sixth round on the seventh day. Once more around and it's going to happen. Don't give up! James strikes the same note in 1:4: 'But let patience have its perfect work, that you may be perfect and complete, lacking nothing.' Unless we are patient and allow perseverance to finish its work, faith will be incomplete, the faith process will abort and we will not receive the promise. James then exposes what can so easily enter in at this point to rob us of the promise of faith. He says, 'Be careful not to let doubt or double-mindedness enter in.' These things bring about the instability that can capsize our faith. We become tossed about like a wave of the sea blown here and there by the fickle winds of opposition. We soon lose our course and end up beached many miles from where we want to be. Seafarers set their course and follow it until they reach their destination; and on the journey of faith, so must we. Entertaining doubt is like sailing in a leaky vessel, it soon loses its stability and becomes difficult to steer. Finally it becomes uncontrollable and impossible to keep afloat. If we allow double-mindedness to weaken our faith, we become unstable, not knowing where we are going or what God really wants to do with us. And yet, if we keep our faith afloat, we will be able to go wherever God directs, and we will reach our destination.

True faith is buoyant, like a cork riding a storm that sinks ocean liners. It keeps popping up no matter how many times it is pushed down. That kind of faith is in us: the Holy Spirit has made sure of that. I am not talking about our natural, human disposition, although we all know people who seem to have champagne in their personality. They are naturally effervescent and nothing seems to bother them. The world could be collapsing and they would pop up somewhere still bubbling over. Faith is not a matter of human temperament but a spiritual quality that overcomes the world. By God's grace no matter how many times our faith is suppressed, knocked down or discouraged it rises again. In short we must believe and keep on believing, and when we've done that, still keep on believing. 'When the going gets tough, the tough get going.' That's a famous dictum in politics, but in the kingdom of God we need to go even further: 'When the going gets tougher, the tougher *keep going*!'

Faith for tough times

In Matthew 24, Jesus speaks about the kind of pressures that are going to increase in the world. I'm not being alarmist, but frankly those pressures are not particularly encouraging to us as Christians. As we look at our Western society, we find that the outer shell of Christianity is crumbling. The days when people just went to church simply because they thought it was a good thing to do are gone. With the outer shell of Christian consensus crumbling, there's going to be increasing conflict between the values of the world and the values of Jesus Christ. And we Christians are the battleground. Jesus reminds us in Matthew 24:12: 'And because lawlessness will abound, the love of many will grow cold.' The great temptation of the hour is to grow cold, but in verse 13 he says, 'But he who endures to the end shall be saved.' We must believe and keep on believing, hold fast and keep on holding fast. Now, I want to share some encouraging parts from Scripture that all show faith is an ongoing experience.

Keep believing

In 1 Peter 1:8–9 Peter says, 'whom having not seen you love. Though now you do not see Him, yet believing, you rejoice with joy inexpressible and full of glory, receiving the end of your faith – the salvation of your souls.' We are receiving because we are believing. This present, ongoing sense of believing, is also stressed in John 1:12 which refers to people who receive Jesus Christ: 'As many as received Him, to them He gave the right to become children of God, to those who believe in His name.' The word 'believe' there is in the present continuous tense. Faith is a present tense activity. It's no good looking back and saying, 'I believed once', we must continue in faith feeding it on a daily basis. We know this world's mentality is rooted in material and visible things, and is hostile to faith, whereas Christians basically build their lives on that which is invisible. So we need to keep our faith fresh.

In John 6:47 Jesus says, 'Most assuredly, I say to you, he who believes in Me has everlasting life.' The word 'believe' there is also in the present continuous tense. It is one who believes, and *keeps on believing*, who has everlasting life. In any matter of faith, you may be able to say you had faith yesterday. But what about today? What about the many promises that God has spoken into our heart that we're not believing any longer? We *had* hoped, we *were* believing but that faith needs to be freshened up. It needs to be revitalised today, so it becomes *a present expression of faith*, believing God today. The Apostle Paul says the same thing in Romans 3:22: 'the righteousness of God, through faith in Jesus Christ, to all and on all who believe.' Again, this is the present continuous tense. It is those who believe and continue to do so that have the righteousness of God. The same is true for every other provision of faith. Unless our faith is maintained, fresh and active each day, it cannot be effective.

Don't throw away your confidence

The entire Book of Hebrews is a rallying call to persist in faith. Hebrews 10:35–6 says, 'Therefore do not cast away your confidence, which has great reward. For you have need of endurance, so that after you have done the will of God, you may receive the promise.' In order to receive the promise there must be perseverance so that when we have done the will of God, we will inherit. There can be no promise without perseverance. We want the ecstasy without the agony, but it doesn't work that way: we have to pay the price. But God encourages us: *persistent faith will be rewarded, it cannot fail*. Every time people came to Jesus in open, honest and persistent faith, he rewarded their faith and blessed them. He never turned anyone empty away.

The gospels tell the story of a woman who had suffered from bleeding for twelve years, but was finally healed by Jesus. This story was a great encouragement to Bola, a young West African mother who attended our church. She suffered from a similar condition and over the course of her seven-year ordeal, clung to the promise of healing she felt was hers through the story from the gospels. Like the woman in the New Testament, she had gone for medical help, but her condition was such that they could only provide partial and temporary relief. Bola's underlying condition grew worse. However, she refused to give up believing that one day the Lord Jesus would heal her. I would often see her at the front of the church receiving prayer for healing, but for years nothing happened.

Then one night she had a remarkable dream. Jesus appeared to her standing over her, and in her dream she felt something happen inside her body: she was healed. In the morning, recollecting the dream, she rushed to the bathroom. Was it real? Had the Lord really touched her in the night? Sure enough, the bleeding had stopped, and she was completely well from that moment. It is so important to hold on to our faith conviction, and never let it go.

The word 'confidence' in Hebrews 10:35 carries the meaning of freedom of speech. It is the kind of freedom of speech that comes from boldness, a complete absence of fear. To put it another way, it is boldness in speech which comes from a fixed sense of confidence and conviction. Bold people speak up, but fearful people keep quiet. We have a deep Spirit-produced confidence and conviction within us. Hold on to that. When God says don't throw it away, he knows our human nature. He doesn't just say, 'Don't let it slip', he says, 'Don't throw it away.' We all have times when we want to take that confidence and throw it away. The tests, the trials, the pressures are too much. Don't throw away your confidence. Treasure it, prize it and keep it alive because it will be richly rewarded.

You may be finding this difficult to put into practice because of the particular problems you are facing. But the Christians addressed in the Book of Hebrews were also having a tough time. They had endured many trials and were rather tender converts. They were still wondering whether they had done the right thing in becoming Christians. The writer to the Hebrews is encouraging them to keep the faith despite their difficulties. They were being persecuted for their faith, had suffered the loss of their property for the sake of Jesus and were in danger of giving up altogether. Confused about their identity they were letting double-mindedness creep in. And so in Hebrews 6:11–12 the writer encourages them, 'You started off very well and I want each of you to show the same diligence to the very end in order to make your hope sure. Imitate those who through faith and perseverance inherit what is promised.'

We don't just inherit through faith, but through faith and *perseverance*. We must turn our suffering into patient endurance before God, waiting for him to act, and he will act. God says, 'show this same diligence to the very end.' Diligence is zealous, active and earnest faith that can be seen. Show this diligence, keep at it, keep doing those works, keep fulfilling the will of God. Don't give in. Keep showing this same diligence, this zealous attitude towards active and earnest faith. Do it to the very end, to the point of securing what you are believing for. Jesus is the author and *finisher* of our faith (Hebrews 12:2), the one who began that good work and who also brings it to completion.

After all, we're not believing on our own. The Lord Jesus is helping us. He is encouraging us, strengthening us and working in us to ensure that we don't miss our inheritance. Jesus himself helps us by the Spirit to forge every link in the chain of faith. The Holy Spirit is called the Spirit of faith (2 Corinthians 4:13), and he helps us throughout the whole process of faith. It is the Spirit who inspires us to believe the Word and by whom we speak the amen to the Word of faith. He helps us to hear, believe, confess and do the Word of God. He helps us to endure faith's tests, inspires us to praise God in the midst of the trial and gives us the persistence to hold on until faith is rewarded. But if for any moment we hold back or give up we are putting the faith process at risk. Let us keep on believing, keep on holding on to the truth and then we will not miss our inheritance.

Living the life of faith is seeking to please God in all things. It pleases him when we take him at his Word and believe him for *all* the provisions he has promised us. This is not a selfish attitude, rather it is honouring God, and showing the world that he loves enough to bless us abundantly, and that we trust him enough to let him do it. There are thousands of promises that God has given us covering every area of life and every need we will ever have. Let us take them by faith, persevere until they become ours.

Let me ask what you are believing God for, right now. Where are you being tempted and tested to give in and say, 'I won't bother believing *that* any more'? We don't have to choose to live a mediocre life, it comes naturally. But the moment we choose to become active for God we are a target of the enemy. That's when the testing really happens and persistence must come through. Jesus is both the author and the finisher of our faith (Hebrews 12:2), the one who both initiates it and completes it. Let him help you persist in faith, taking you through the entire journey step by step until everything is fulfilled.

11   Developing Faith

*By faith Abraham obeyed when he was called to
go out to the place which he would receive as an
inheritance. And he went out, not knowing where
he was going* (Hebrews 11:8).

Throughout this book references have been made to
Abraham, one of the greatest biblical heroes of faith.
It is natural for us to use him as a prototype for the
life of faith. The Bible calls him 'the father of those
that believe'. So it is appropriate to look in detail at
Abraham's faith. In the next four chapters we are going
to see how the principles of faith are demonstrated in
his life, responses and attitudes.

As we do, remember that Abraham, although a great
pioneer of faith was nevertheless human just like us.
He was subject to the same limitations, weaknesses
and had the same struggle to believe God that we
have. His circumstances, personal inability and his
own failures are made very clear in the Word of God.
He met with difficulty and sometimes gave into the
forces opposing his faith. The tragedy of Ishmael is
recorded for all the world to see, and the consequences
of Abraham's mistake are with us today. And yet God
did not reject him, but in grace and patience gradually
perfected the process of faith within him. Abraham
believed, and God acted. This man rose to such heights
of mature, perfected faith that he was prepared to trust
God in what must have been one of the severest tests

anyone has ever had to endure – the sacrifice of Isaac (Genesis 22).

All this may seem so unattainable to us as we face the daily struggle of our lives, but remember, we are *children* of Abraham. The same faith God put into Abraham's heart, he has given to us also. We carry the family characteristic as we follow in the footsteps of faithful Abraham.

Faith is redemptive

The story of faith is about God's desire to save us and reveal his love to us as the drama of salvation is played out in the lives of countless saints of numerous generations. People who heard God and believed him, who trusted God and acted on their faith. Nowhere is this more apparent than with Abraham. He is the prototype believer, the great example of what it means to be justified by faith, placed by grace on a right standing with God through faith. Even the cross, so central to the plan of salvation, is epitomised in his life as he, to all intents and purposes, sacrifices his son, and is prophetically announced from the summit of the mountain of sacrifice with the words 'God will provide for Himself the lamb for a burnt offering' (Genesis 22:8).

Our faith too treads the same path of redemption that stretches from Abraham to today. And the link is the cross of Christ on Mount Calvary. True faith follows the trail of Christ's blood to the crucifixion of Christ, the sacrificial Lamb of God. Today, every step of faith we take is the telling of the same story, and the unfolding of the same theme of salvation. And this is not simply the receiving of a ticket to heaven, for the 'just shall *live* by faith'.

Saving faith rightfully relates to the future, in assurance of what will be ours in the *future* life, but it also lays hold of all God's promises for *today*. Like a motion picture faith is lived one frame at a time. Each snapshot catches a moment of faith, a decision to believe God and follow him. In this world of flickering, often menacing, shadows it is only a life of faith that carries reality and superimposes God's reality onto the pretence that we call the real world. Not one moment of faith is wasted as God writes that reality into our lives.

Like Abraham we must learn many lessons of faith that carry implications far beyond our own lives. No matter how intensely satisfying faith may be to our own personal desires, as the Giving God meets our many needs, faith holds promise beyond ourselves for the good of others and the greater glory of God himself.

The call

Faith initiates nothing. It can only call back in response to God. Faith can only respond to grace. It all began when 'The God of glory appeared to our father Abraham when he was in Mesopotamia, before he dwelt in Haran' (Acts 7:2). This was God's call to Abraham. Before that, there is no reason to believe that he was a holy man or that he was even seeking God. In fact, he had no knowledge of God at all and was probably a pagan idolator along with the rest of his generation.

I once saw in the British Museum various ancient tablets showing what the Babylonian religious beliefs were during Abraham's time in Ur of the Chaldees. They worshipped gods represented by the moon, the

sun and the stars. But now the God who created these
things was revealing himself to Abraham, or Abram as
he was called then. The Creator was speaking to one
who, up to that point, had no knowledge beyond the
blindness of idolatry, the worship of created things.

Needless to say, such an encounter, however it happened, was life-transforming. Suddenly all Abram's
values were turned upside down. Faith is like that. It
has a way of <u>reversing everything</u>. What we previously
believed, we no longer believe. What we felt most sure
of, now is as nothing in the light of God's revealed
truth. What we held as factual certainties are now
challenged to their very foundations. We realise that
we were building on sand. All this comes with the call
of God. We did not attain to it, it came to us, not as
human discovery but divine revelation. Faith sets us
apart. It changes our priorities. When God calls, and
we recognise the reality behind that call, all we can
do is respond to it. We do not initiate it, but we must
obey it.

All change!

For Abram, the immediate challenge was, 'Get out of
your country, from your family and from your father's
house, to a land that I will show you' (Genesis 12:1).
This is always the first challenge of faith. *There has
to be a leaving behind and a going forth*. The shift
is not necessarily a change of location but faith
always demands radical change. There is the change
of direction that the Bible calls repentance. It is acting
in the light of the truth given to you. Then there are
the changes that come through advancing in spiritual
things. You cannot move forward while staying in the
same place. God calls you out of the comfort zone to

break free from the familiar into the new, the strange, the unfamiliar. This is always the cost of the adventure of faith.

I was born in East Africa, grew up in Australia and lived most of my life in Britain. This, together with an annual diary that takes me all over the world, has made me aware of people who are not living in their place of origin. Immigrants, expatriates and displaced peoples all know firsthand the mental, emotional and psychological upheaval that accompanies a move from one land to another. This is most acute when you are a refugee and do not know where your home will be. God called Abram to that commitment. And, as the New Testament records, 'By faith Abraham obeyed . . . and he went out, not knowing where he was going' (Hebrews 11:8).

Trust factor

In the interests of faith, God who knows the end from the beginning does not always show the end from the beginning. Faith knows a destiny not a destination. It is a journey, taken step by step, with usually only enough light to take the next step. God gives the general direction, a sense of purpose and calls for trusting obedience. That is how he works out his plan.

But why doesn't he reveal more and give us greater chunks of understanding to go by? In all of this God is dealing with us lovingly and graciously. Jesus, in the upper room just before his departure, said to his disciples, 'I still have many things to say to you, but you cannot bear them now' (John 16:12). So the Father knows that we can only handle so much information, particularly about the future. Thank God we only know so much. I can think of many situations in my life which

if I had known in advance were going to happen, would
have only added to my anxiety. God is justified in
dealing with us on a need-to-know basis.

Also, the whole intention of a life of faith is to
develop such a relationship of trust with God that we
are content to trust him with our very lives. It is only
the independence and self-determining within us that
demands to know 'Why?' or 'How long?' or 'After
this?' We do not know the future, but we do know
who holds it and who will guide us through it. So if
God appears to be withholding information from you,
remember he is calling for trust. Faith without trust is
like a house, fully furnished but without occupants,
technically a home, but empty and wasted, not fulfilling
its real purpose.

Battle of obedience

In Genesis 11:31, we read of Abram's surprising
move to Haran. At first sight it seems as if it was
in response to the command of God to leave his
home and his country, an act of obedience. But a
closer look shows the real battle going on in Abram's
life. It is encouraging to see the inner struggles Bible
characters often experience. We often wrongly assume
that because these people appear on the sacred pages
they must have been near perfect examples of believing
saints, or that somehow it was easy for them. This tends
to discourage real progress in our lives because we
think there must have been something special about
these people. Nothing could be further from the truth,
especially for Abram.

The record shows the move as originating from
Terah, Abram's father. Did this mean Abram was
still under the influence of his father, and did not

feel free to obey God's Word? Did he first have to convince his father before he could do it? And what about the other directive to leave his family and his father's house? What tensions did this cause? It is often true that God's Word to us cuts across the plans others have for us, particularly our closest friends and relatives. Apart from the obvious conflict this brings, the potential for misunderstanding of the nature and heart of God is enormous.

But the life of faith cannot be compromised. God's kingdom, his plans and will must come before even the best intentions of ours and others near to us. When you truly hear from God, no matter what additional wisdom can be gleaned from close advisers and counsellors, God's Word must remain. Obedience is the only acceptable response. And for Abram, the battle was on. The move from Ur of the Chaldeans was with the intention of going into Canaan, but the family stopped short at Haran. It was an impressive move, clearly in response to the revelation received, but it was not full obedience. Haran was still in the region of Mesopotamia. They had *not* left that land! They had come only as far as they possibly could without doing so. This was bogus obedience and false faith. It looked good, could pass for the real thing, but was not what God had directed. Sadly this is where they settled.

Not far enough

It is where much of the Christian Church lives, and where we spend most of our lives. We take faith so far, and no further. We go far enough to make it look as if we are serious about obeying God, but still fall short of actually doing what God says. But *real faith goes all the way*. We give God fine talk, but we often are void of action. Instead of real action we offer him mere activity, hiding our disobedience under a mass of meetings, committees, conferences and seminars. Take evangelism, for example. We acknowledge that Jesus commands us to do it. We talk about it, study it, make surveys about it, preach and pray about it, but we don't actually do it! As we have seen, faith means nothing less than doing the Word.

Finally, Abram did obey God, although it was not until his father had passed away and been buried in Haran. Until that moment of obedience to the Word of God, Abram could develop his faith no further. Perhaps, he, like his father, would have died on the border of the adventure into the impossible that lay ahead. He would never have fulfilled his personal destiny. But he was now ready to carry forward the purposes of God. Obedience opened the way for the fulfilment of the promise.

Shortly after I had finished the first part of my theological training, I was looking for the next step in Christian service. I had left my life in the theatre two years before and I was sure that God had something special planned for me to do for him. But what was it? Before my call into the Christian ministry I had been challenged by the needs of people addicted to drugs and had spent as much time as I could befriending these street people. The drug culture of the 1960s had left its toll and many young people in the mid-1970s were picking up the tab.

An opening was possible at the drug and alcohol Christian rehabilitation centre which at that time was attached to Kensington Temple. I was not sure if this step was the right one for me to take. I was sure that it was a worthwhile job, but not so sure how it fitted into my overall gifts and calling in God's work. I had these things on my mind when I attended a small group fellowship meeting one evening. A prophecy was given which went something like this: 'Before you is a door. It is small and insignificant and many would pass it by. But as you go through it you will find another door. This one is very wide and it will open up to you wonderful paths of service that are now unimaginable to you.'

I knew at once that this was a word for me and obeyed the Lord, spending two years in hard, practical service in the drugs home. I learned a great deal and, to this day, value my time there. This position led on to a job as a church worker in Kensington Temple and ultimately into the pastorate. Since then my ministry has taken me all over the world and I have truly seen the most wonderful things happen, that as the Lord said, I could never have imagined when I obeyed the call to rehabilitation work. Obeying that simple word from the Lord was the key to it all.

12   The Promise

*For if the inheritance is of the law, it is no
longer of promise; but God gave it to Abraham
by promise* (Galatians 3:18).

Faith is according to promise, not law. It corresponds
as closely to promise as works correspond to law. Faith
works by grace, not by human effort. What a tragedy
that today many people's faith has been snared in the
trap of legalism. Faith's principles have been reduced
to laws and slick formulae, mere push-button religion.
Law chokes faith because it cuts off its life-supply.
Grace is the only thing that feeds faith and keeps it
alive. Law evokes self-effort and spawns defeat and
guilt, the twin enemies of faith. Grace spotlights Christ
and his achievements, encouraging faith to lay hold of
his victory. Fleshly effort has no place in the life of
faith. God calls for trust in the promise of his Word.
Law sets up other conditions for blessing, conditions
that we cannot keep and so the result is cursing.

You could not find anyone more disillusioned than
the man or woman who has been damaged by legalism
in the matter of faith: those who have been wrongly
told that God will only bless if you first perform. This
is totally against the Gospel of Christ who does not
expect you first to master laws whether they be the
Ten Commandments or the 'laws of faith'.

The Apostle Paul in using Abraham's experience
as the pattern of Gospel faith says that the promise

given to Abraham and his descendants depended on the response of faith and not the obedience of law: 'Therefore it is of faith that it might be according to grace, so that the promise might be sure to all the seed . . .' (Romans 4:16). Abraham's blessing depended on the promise made to him, not his efforts. God will bless you because in love he has promised it. He will keep his promise to you despite your inability to reach his standards. And in responding to this work of his grace, God himself transforms you from within so that you are being conformed into the likeness of what he wants you to become. So it was for Abraham, and so it is for all his seed.

But it is this unconditional promise to bless that we find so hard to accept; after all, it has no parallel in our experience. Not even any other religion offers such unconditional love bestowed on man by God, the Master of the universe. However, God's nature is to bless, and the promise is for blessing: 'I will bless you and make your name great' (Genesis 12:2). God wants to bless people and lift them up; the devil pulls them down. Smith Wigglesworth said, 'Most people's God is my devil.' He was commenting on the predisposition of the religious mind to project onto God the misery and pain that in real biblical terms comes from the enemy. Yet somehow we grow up with such a negative view of God that faith can barely function. How can we believe God to lift the suffering we think he is causing in the first place?

Much of traditional Christianity is overshadowed by negative images of drab buildings and dismal people with certainly no 'good news' look about them. I am speaking from experience. As a young student in London, recently awakened to the uncertainties of life by my father's death, I searched in vain for God in some of the churches of London. I may have been unfortunate in looking in the churches that do not preach the Word in its simplicity, uncluttered by man-made ideas. I now know that there are many fine churches in our capital city, but they should *all* be fine, ready to present a faith that is real in a God who is real; a God who is ready and always willing to bless; a good God who wants good things for his people; a God who will gladly meet us at our point of personal need, no matter how big or seemingly insignificant that need may be.

God is not the forbidding Lawmaker and Judge that he is distorted to be, neither is he the Father Christmas caricature as some present him. He is the righteous and holy Father, who loves to give and has, in Christ, opened up the door to his blessing without compromising his holiness or his righteousness. God is a good God who wills good things and works good things. He is not one to withhold. He has already given everything in giving us his Son; how can he withhold now? His offer of blessing comes despite the risk of rejection and abuse of his goodness.

Abram's faith was founded on the certain conviction that God was ready to bless him. Some adopt a position which is more spiritual than God himself! Once more it is the working of the religious mind fostering false notions, false humility. They say that the gifts conceal the Giver, because we are inclined to seek God's provision rather than God himself. In fact, they do the opposite, the gifts *reveal* the Giver. Those who truly receive God's blessing know the true Heart behind them. They open up to his love, and are thankful, and they are changed. We are all the more encouraged to seek his face when we know it is smiling. When the tender hand of God touches us in blessing, we are drawn closer to him. His goodness melts our selfishness and hardness of heart. God knows what he is doing and he will never over-indulge his children.

Faith and character

The life of faith, despite its rewards, carries no promise of blessing without character development, of communion without cost. God is too good a Father to let that happen. Faith is our entrance into the school of his discipline, and he has his own way of purifying our motives. Like Job, we will be tested. Along with the blessings come the trials. The trouble is some attempt to do the work of God for him. In a perverse form of superspirituality they preach a gospel of misery, coming from a God who inflicts sickness, but never heals, except through medicine or under very rare circumstances. They make out that to be truly spiritual you have to be poor and miserable. You can never presume that God wants to improve your lot in life. Happiness in the hereafter; but for now, just grit your teeth!

I know that there is the equal and opposite danger of becoming 'blessings crazy'. There is no superficiality worse than that of serving God for what we think we can get out of him, or trying to live as if suffering was never a part of this life and that God's sole commitment is to our present comfort. This is selfish living: it is not Christianity. It has nothing to do with the Christ who carried the cross and commands us to do the same. That is why true faith centres on the cross. It acknowledges that the price has been paid, once for all. It is religion that demands we keep on paying even when Christ has declared, 'It is finished!' (John 19:30). Faith also acknowledges that the blessings flowing from the cross have a long distance to travel before they are fully delivered and become part of our lives. The full manifestation is ahead; God is preparing that for us in heaven. But faith never doubts the goodness of God, not for one second. It lays hold of God, receives his blessings and lives in total dependence on him.

The confirmation

Believing God is an ongoing process. Like a pattern being woven into fabric, it takes time to discern the design emerging from the apparent tangles. It is also like a pregnancy. First comes conception, then forty weeks of gestation, before there is a travail and a bringing forth. Faith is a gradual and fragile process which at any point may be aborted. But God is faithful in overseeing the whole process and providing at every point just what is needed to complete it.

Some time into this process, Abram's faith began to fail. The promise had not been fulfilled; in fact, it seemed more far off than ever. He was discouraged and at an all-time low. He found it difficult to believe that God was ever going to do anything for him, let alone fulfil his words 'I will make you a great nation' (Genesis 12:2). A great nation? Sure, he had experienced something of God's blessing but the central promise was nowhere to be seen. Sarah was still barren. How could this childless and rapidly ageing man become the patriarch of a great nation? To human thinking it was just not possible.

In times of difficulty the devil's temptation to doubt the Word is strong. You can be sure the devil will tempt you to deny what God has said and he will use every means available. What's the difference between this and what God does in allowing circumstances which so convincingly contradict his Word? In short, the devil tempts us to destroy our faith, but God tests our faith in order to develop it. The devil will cause doubt to overtake us by questioning or contradicting God's Words or by slandering God's character. God's tests direct us away from the raging circumstances towards the security of his unchanging Word and his promise. In the midst of the trial he confirms his Word. The quiet confidence we have when all around appears to collapse comes from the inner conviction that God has spoken.

It was this conviction that Abram needed to find again; and the confirmation came. The same Word spoken by God in the beginning was spoken a second time. God had not forgotten. His Word to Abram was as fresh before him and his promise was as real as it was when it was first spoken. This is the enduring nature of God's Word. It is living. It carries the life-giving breath of God. It cannot die. It is eternal. It cannot fail. It is all powerful. The Word of God carries within it the ability to see its own complete fulfilment. We may forget God's Word but it is ever before him. It stands eternal in the heavens, immovable. We may doubt it, but that does not for one moment diminish its power.

But notice how God confirms his Word to Abram. He does it by pointing to himself, to the trustworthiness of his Person and the integrity of his character. 'After these things the word of the Lord came to Abram in a vision, saying, "Do not be afraid, Abram. I am your shield, your exceedingly great reward"' (Genesis 15:1).

God was saying, 'Abram, you can trust me. I will not fail you. You will receive the reward of your faith.' But he was also pointing out to Abram the true nature of the reward: 'Abram, look to Me – I am your reward.' *We distort faith if we think its object is anything other than God himself*. In the final analysis, all that God really promises is himself. Every promise flows from him and leads back to him. Faith can never come to maturity until this lesson is learned. Even the most spectacular gift or blessing from God, for example some dramatic healing, is simply a revelation of God's character. When God blesses, he gives of himself and when we receive his gifts and benefits we receive him.

I have often found that when people receive some physical blessing or special answer to prayer, it is not so much what they get from God but it is their experience of him that blesses them most. During a very special time of public worship, a young woman called Jane felt the Lord's touch in her body. She had been troubled by a lump that had recently appeared in her breast. It was causing considerable discomfort and she could feel the pain deep into her armpit. She was due to have tests at the hospital. After the time of worship, Jane was astonished to find not only the pain, but the lump completely gone from her breast. She was overjoyed and could not get over the feelings of love that seemed to envelop her. This love was an even greater miracle to her than her healing.

Just how much Abram needed a confirmation of God's love is shown by his response. He said, 'Lord God, what will You give me, seeing I go childless, and the heir of my house is Eliezer of Damascus? Look, You have given me no offspring; indeed one born in my house is my heir!' (Genesis 15:2–3). He challenges God outright. But this is baby faith talking, with so much yet to learn and, as yet, unready to receive from God. But we sympathise with Abram; after all, how would we have reacted? When God's promises seem slow in coming, don't we get just as impatient, just as frustrated?

I have often heard people say, 'God is not in a hurry – he's never late!' As a person who understands punctuality, I can appreciate that God would never be late. But my problem is that he is never early! I find myself grappling with this question of God's timing again and again. Why is it that God often appears late and never comes early? Because he is always on time. He is the master of precision timing. Too early and we are not ready, too late and we are finished. I think this aspect of faith holds the greatest potential for the development of our character. We must also bear in mind that it is often *we* who delay God's purposes, frustrating them by our unbelief.

God knows exactly how to let faith do its perfect work in us. When human hope is lost and human efforts fail, faith takes over. True faith relates to what God alone can do. It has nothing to do with man's efforts or ability. Had God brought the promise to Abram too early it would not have been such an obvious miracle or vehicle of faith. The promise only came when all human hope was gone, when Abram's own body was dead, at least in terms of fathering a child. Then and only then could God demonstrate that faith was the only answer and that what had happened was nothing to do with anything that could be explained naturally.

This does not contradict the principle of faith's action that I developed in chapter seven. There is an action of faith that exactly corresponds to every promise of faith. What an act of faith it was for old Abraham and Sarah. A barren woman and a sterile man engaging in sexual relations in order to produce a child, because they believed God despite their physical circumstances. However, at this time faith was not that strong and Abram's accusation was, 'Look, you have not done what you promised.' But God's loving response was a reiteration of his Word of assurance, 'one who will come from your own body shall be your heir' (Genesis 15:4). Possibly Abram had given up on the promise altogether and was going to adopt one of his servants, making him the heir of his entire estate. This tendency to give God a helping hand and hurry the fulfilment along was to get Abram into great difficulty later on. But in spite of it all, Abram's life was in God's hands and he was not about to let it fall to the ground. God's capacity is endless, and when we flag and fail, he remains strong.

Faith is a partnership which flows from a relationship between God and us by the power of the Holy Spirit. The initiative is God's, for faith can initiate nothing, and we are totally dependent on his gracious nature. God's generosity overflows from a great heart of love and touches our lives. Faith then makes the response to what God has already set in motion. That is the partnership, and it was the basis of Abram's life of faith.

One of the strongest misconceptions surrounding the subject of faith is that it comes, pre-packaged and fully-formed; that is simply not the case. Faith must grow, develop, and come to maturity; it must be perfected. That is where the relational aspect of faith comes into focus. Our whole relationship with God is one of faith. Growing in our relationship with God means growing in faith, and in that relationship God is fully committed to seeing *our* faith develop.

That is how he dealt with Abram. This would-be father of the faithful was in need of tutoring. He was struggling to believe. The promise had been made clear, in the beginning: 'I will make you a father of nations'; but now it seemed far off, perhaps never to be realised. Abram's reaction is familiar to us all, for it has been ours many times, when we have attempted to venture into the life of faith. God says something, we believe it at one level; but the tests come, and we cave in. We heard God speak, but nothing has changed, the promise has not materialised. Instead, the evidence of the physical world – the one we really know, based on facts that you can see, taste, touch, smell and hear with our physical senses – dulls our perception of spiritual matters. The biblical order, 'believing is seeing', becomes the all too familiar 'seeing is believing', and as far as we can see, *nothing* has happened, and characteristically things get worse and worse.

That is when we ask ourselves, 'Was it really God, or my imagination? Faith or wishful thinking? Presumptuous dreaming?' We cannot ignore psychology here: the human personality is prone to wish fulfilment. Who has not seen the tragedy of those who deny facts too horrible to face and cling to empty hopes. Without letting the Word and the Spirit work a foundation for faith, the hasty conclusion is clutched from the air in order to bring emotional relief from reality: 'God has told me! Look, here is the verse!' And yet this psychological self-persuasion is not enough and soon reality sets in cold and hard, like concrete.

But that is not true faith. *Faith is not convincing yourself; it is being convinced by God*, his Word and his Spirit. That is why it is so important to understand the process of faith. It must grow like seed: first the green shoots, then the fuller stem and leaves and finally comes the full plant, bearing the marks of maturity – the promise fulfilled and fruit that remains.

However, some guard against psychological faith so carefully that they lose out altogether. It is as though they are unable to face the disappointment of believing and being let down. This can have a refined theological and religious face. A new strange world is constructed around the believer in the name of God. In this world, suffering is a virtue and fulfilment is illegitimate. The will of God, therefore, is to promote the one and to disallow the other. However, it is a creed beyond practice because, except for a few religious ascetics or hermits, we all live by another rule. We try to avoid or alleviate suffering through medicine, education and financial provision. We seek the normal satisfactions of life and pursue goodness on this basic level. The result is that God is pushed out of our lives and we try to make it all work by ourselves. That is not faith; it is a perversion of the truth. God is a good God, he wills good things for us, and although he is big enough to use whatever comes our way for our good and his glory, he does not directly will suffering, or injury or sickness in our lives because, as James says, 'Every good gift and every perfect gift is from above, and comes down from the Father of lights, with whom there is no variation or shadow of turning' (James 1:17). I cannot wait until the Western world wakes up to the reality of the devil; at least God will stop getting the blame for everything that goes wrong!

God's promises to Abram were good, along the line of this man's own desires for himself. Abram longed to have a son. In that society at that time, such a longing was almost inevitable. The promise of power, influence and material wealth was also good. Abram wanted these things and was not judged unspiritual for it. But the life of faith is not simply a matter of material benefit. God's purposes went well beyond these things, and he could not have as his patriarch one who was pampered by instant gratification and weak in faith. That is why we cannot expect God to give to immature faith. There were other matters beyond the wishes of one man, even Abram. The delay was no delay at all and totally deliberate on God's part. He was developing a man of character, a man of God.

13 The Covenant

*For by one offering He has perfected forever those
who are being sanctified* (Hebrews 10:14).

Reinhard Bonnke, the well-known German evangelist,
is a great inspiration to those seeking to grow in faith.
Whenever you spend time with him you always come
away with renewed confidence that God is able to do
whatever he promises to do. For Reinhard, the lessons
in the school of faith have been long and hard. In the
early days he had a big heart to reach the lost of Africa,
but his ministry did not rise to it. As a young preacher in
the tiny Southern African nation of Lesotho, he did not
attract the crowds his ministry does today. In answer to
his heart cry God sent Reinhard visions in the night. He
saw a blood-washed Africa and heard the words 'Africa
shall be saved.' This formed the basis of a new ministry
of evangelism that has swept across Africa with up to
half a million people in a single meeting.

Europe too is ripe for the evangelistic harvest, where
fruitful ministries of faith and power are also emerging.
But whether our call is to large-scale evangelism or to
reach the individuals who are touched by our lives in
our home or neighbourhood, faith in God's Word is
essential. And the most important lesson of faith is
that God's Word is enough. But God knows exactly
what we need to encourage us and to bring our faith
to maturity. As God did for the young Reinhard in our
day, in ancient times he drove the same lesson home

to the dispirited Abram with a powerful visual aid. God
came to Abram when he was at an extremely low point,
struggling to believe the promise. He took him outside
the tent and directed his eyes heavenward, toward the
stars which pierced the night sky. 'Count them, if you
can', God said. 'So shall your descendants be.'

God knows the power of vision and he lifted Abram
above the earthly into the higher realm, and there he
saw the stars that he used to worship along with the
sun and the moon. Then the realisation came to him.
He now knew and worshipped the God who made them
all. He understood that God's power has no limits. God
has power to back up his Word and no promise of his
can fail for lack of his ability to keep it. Abram's faith
took a quantum leap forward. It was as real as if he
could see in the heavens the smiling faces of every one
of his future children, and as if he heard them calling
him, 'Daddy!'

Beyond the visible

That the Word came in such a powerful visual form was
a wonderful accommodation to the human mindset.
Pictures are often more powerful than words. The
message conveyed becomes real and concrete, less
abstract and less distant; consequently, we are able
to grasp it better. Before we understand a principle
and are able to take it in, we usually need to see it
in our mind, or carry it in our heart.

God gave Abram the image for him to carry permanently in his mind's eye. He was not introducing
Abram to the techniques of occultic visualisation
inviting him to create his own reality. It was a godly
way of seeing beyond the visible to the invisible realm
of faith. You will never see the promises with your

eyes until you see them with your faith. God used
the picture of the stars to stimulate Abram's faith.
He will often work in a similar way with us, using
what we know and understand to help us grasp the
invisible and the impossible that lies beyond it. There
is no artificial technique here, but the Holy Spirit will
often give you something concrete to take hold of, in
the process of faith. It may be a picture, a word or
an idea, but it stimulates your faith and anchors it in
the concrete. Faith deals with the specific rather than
with the vague and abstract generalisations of truth.
Understanding what the promise will look like when
it comes is a vital part of the process of faith.

I am not suggesting that this is a technique which we
can use to manufacture faith. Rather, it is an integral
part of the operation of faith itself. Faith is the capacity
to see the fulfilment *before* it is visible. In fact, when
it comes to the promises of God, you will never see
with your natural eyes what you do not first see with
the eyes of faith. If you possess real faith, it will be as
if you can see it, touch it and handle it *before it actually
appears in the physical realm*. And so, when you are
seeking God for the fulfilment of some promise, allow
the Holy Spirit to show you, through the eyes of faith,
what that fulfilment will look like. The Holy Spirit will
bring you a very clear 'faith picture' of the reality you
are believing for. Faith is very specific.

Suddenly the promise of God became real and faith
entered Abram's spirit; not that he didn't believe
God before, but it reached new levels. Both the
Old Testament and New Testament record this as
the moment of faith for Abram, the beginning of
his life of righteousness: 'And he believed in the
Lord, and He accounted it to him for righteousness'
(Genesis 15:6; Romans 4:3). The greatest tests still lay
ahead, and faith was a long way from reaching full

maturity. There was to be significant failure ahead and many lessons still to be learned, but Abram began to believe.

This makes what happened next all the more astonishing. Faith needs honing and refining; it must grow. Straight away God moved to another part of the promise as if to take Abram on to the next stage of his faith development. He reiterated his Word about the land: 'I am the Lord, who brought you out of Ur of the Chaldeans to give you this land to inherit it' (Genesis 15:7). Faith never stops short of the full promise. *We* can settle for second best, but *God* never does. He fulfils his total purpose. The inheritance of the land had to do with promises beyond Abram as an individual or his lifetime. God reminded him that he had brought him out of Ur and into Canaan, in order to possess it.

Abram's reply appears strange coming from a man who receives several commendations in Scripture for the faith he held at this point. He said, 'How shall I know that I will inherit?' (Genesis 15:8). Was this a sudden lapse of faith? Was Abram now questioning that which he had so recently gained? I don't think so. Abram was learning the language of faith. Instinctively, he felt for an assurance beyond himself. He did not doubt the Word or the promise. God is as good as his Word, but the revelation was unfolding. There was one major element missing, and Abram, perhaps unknowingly, calls for it.

Faith calls for covenant

Sensing his own weakness, Abram wondered how his faith would endure, and how, with all his human inability to believe, he would make it to the end. It was a cry of conscience: 'How shall I know that *I* shall inherit it?' He knew that the answer depended not on his own strength or ability, but on a source outside himself. True faith looks away from self to the assurance that comes from God alone. Whether Abram understood it or not, he was actually asking for a covenantal guarantee. A covenant is a contract, a binding guarantee. They were commonplace in the ancient world, as they are today. Everything from marriage to politics was governed by contracts, binding agreements between people. These covenants took many forms, but the one detailed in Genesis chapter 15 was a form of blood covenant and is central to our understanding of the whole nature of faith.

God responded to Abram's call for assurance by setting up a covenant in which he bound himself irrevocably to fulfil his Word. Now this was entirely an act of grace on God's part. He did not need to do this to keep his Word: that was guaranteed already. God's Word is enough. It is his bond. But grace, by nature, fits itself exactly to man's true need, and although God did not need this covenant, Abram did. As a result, he had a double guarantee – God's Word, and his covenantal promise to keep it.

The nature of blood covenant

There were various types of blood covenant in Abram's time, but this one was made in the following manner. Several animals and birds were killed and cut in two, and the pieces were placed on the ground, with the halves opposite each other. In its full form, both parties entering the covenant would pass between the broken bits of animals. This was the covenant oath or pledge and it sealed the terms of the contract, setting it in force.

It was binding on both parties from that moment. The broken pieces of dead animals meant that each party was promising on pain of death to fulfil their part of the covenant. As they walked between the blood-soaked pieces, they were saying to each other, 'If I break my word to you, let me become as one of these animals.' In the event of breach of covenant, the other party, his family and all close to him were free to exact the penalty. It was a blood covenant.

Imagine what was going through Abram's mind as he waited in the darkness on that night. He knew exactly what the dead animals meant. He had laid the pieces out exactly as God had instructed him. Now in the stillness of the night he waited. Dare he think it? Was it possible? Could God, this God who created the sun, the moon and the stars, be coming to make covenant with him?

Suddenly, out of the darkness came the light. A fire, like a smoking oven, a burning torch, dim and distant at first, then closer and closer, it came. The presence he knew, the glory he had seen before, but never quite like this. Transfixed in awe, Abram stood as the incredible happened before his eyes. God passed between those pieces. He was saying, 'If I break my Word to you, may I become as these dead, blood-stained pieces. Abram, that's how you shall know you will inherit the land.' Abram was not invited to walk between the pieces: there was no need. It was a unilateral covenant, all of grace. God took the initiative. He made the promise and all Abram could do was watch and respond by believing and trusting.

No one with a knowledge of the New Testament could fail to see the striking similarity between this scene and that of another, some two thousand years later, when God also came to make a covenant. This time he came, not as a fire, but as a man. He came in the person of his Son, Jesus Christ, as God incarnate. Jesus did not just pass through the broken pieces, but he *himself* became the broken pieces. The blood of the New Covenant is the blood of Jesus, and what Abram had cried out for all those years earlier was gloriously fulfilled on the cross. Only the cross satisfies faith, for faith calls for the cleansing of man's conscience. We cannot rise to the standard, we cannot make it. How can *we know* we shall inherit? Only the blood of Jesus can cleanse the guilty conscience and assure it of God's goodness.

Out of the darkness surrounding the cross, Jesus cried from a body, broken and bloodied, as had been foreshadowed centuries before. He cried, 'It is finished!' (John 19:30). Our faith resonates with that cry because, as we now know, the price has been paid. We can inherit the promises of God! Faith embraces that finished work and rejoices. The blood of Christ binds God in covenant agreement. His promises are written and sealed in blood. Only the blood satisfies the human conscience. Only the blood satisfies the justice of God. For it is we who have sinned and fall short of the glory of God, but on the cross Jesus Christ became sin and fully carried its consequences for us. We are free, the covenant is in motion, and the inheritance is ours.

That is why the blood is so important to a life of faith. Without it we cower under the condemnation of certain death; we do not qualify for the inheritance. But with the blood of Christ shed, we are fit to receive, and sit under God's certain guarantee that his Word shall be fulfilled. God sets himself to keep his Word, and the blood is the guarantee. The blood of Christ binds the Father to keep his Word. We have the double witness – the Word of God and the blood of the covenant. The Word is sealed by the blood. Paul puts it like this: 'He who did not spare His own Son, but delivered Him up for us all, how shall He not with Him also freely give us all things?' (Romans 8:32).

Arthur, a young minister, was moving out in the healing ministry, but having difficulty breaking through. He was in earnest as he tried to find out how to encourage people to receive from the Lord. It was the realisation that everything has been accomplished at the cross that finally gave him the release he was looking for. He began to understand that just as we are saved by trusting in the finished work of Christ at Calvary, we are also healed through the same means. He is now growing in the ministry of the Spirit. God has sealed every one of his promises to us in the blood of Christ. He has already given us everything in giving us his Son; this is the full assurance of faith. But there is still one further witness to help us.

The Spirit of faith

Faith has the Word and the blood, but there is more. So far the emphasis has been on the external witnesses and pledge; but faith is even more assured than that. God has given us his Holy Spirit to help in the life of faith. He is called the Spirit of faith (2 Corinthians 4:13). The Spirit always works with the Word and the Spirit always answers to the blood. We do not know whether Abram understood much of these matters, but we do know that without the power of the Spirit he would never have come through. The New Testament states that the blessing of Abraham includes the Spirit of God, and the same promise is given to those who believe in Christ, Abraham's seed. Christ shed his blood on the cross so 'That the blessing of Abraham might come upon the Gentiles in Christ Jesus, that we might receive the promise of the Spirit through faith' (Galatians 3:14).

The third leg of the stool on which faith rests secure is in place, the Holy Spirit our Helper. The promise of the inheritance has been made by Christ, the *Testator*, who died to set it in motion. Then he rose from the dead to become *Executor* of the will, and lives within us by his Spirit to make sure we as *beneficiaries* receive it in full. The Holy Spirit works within us prompting and assuring all the way, as he bears witness to the Word and the blood from within our hearts.

A life of faith is a Spirit-filled life, under the control and direction of the Third Person of the Trinity. Walking in the Spirit and being led by the Spirit is living by faith. The Holy Spirit enables us to take hold of the promises of God by making them real to us and applying them to our particular situation. It is not a matter of laying hold of some formula and following it mechanically; it is a relationship with the Spirit. He quickens the Word and applies the blood, and the promise explodes into life. He gives us the boldness to ask and the courage to stay the course when the endurance test is under way.

Beyond failure

The next episode in Abram's journey of faith is both the worst moment for him and the best for us. It is good for us not because we take pleasure in his failure, but because it offers us hope for our mistakes and an example of what God can do despite our human weakness. I don't know if I am overstating it, but I don't think you can have success without failure. To deny this would be to say you were perfect. The moment you set foot on the road of faith, you enter the possibility of failing in some way. After all in our sinful human nature, we are not perfectly able to hear and to obey God. But he is patient with us and knows the way back. This neither excuses sin, nor prizes the security of inactivity. It is always those in the boat who criticise the Peters out on the water.

Fleshly impatience

Abram once again grew weary of waiting. He believed that God was going to give him an heir. He knew it was going to come from his own body. He knew it was not by adopting Eliezer of Damascus. Previous interviews with God had dealt with those issues. But he was not getting any younger: time was running out. Expectation turned to impatience and Abram once again tried to fulfil the promise his own way, this time in keeping with the Lord's Word: 'the one who will come from your own body will be your heir'. Abram and his wife devised a plan to raise up an heir by their own efforts. Abram had a son by Hagar, Sarai's Egyptian maid. Thus subtle compromise crept in. Abram appears to have thought he was fulfilling the promise, for after Ishmael was born he longed for God to bless him as the heir of the promise. 'Oh, that Ishmael might live before you!' he said.

The road to faith is littered with a thousand Ishmaels, sons born out of the effort of the flesh, yet with spiritual intentions. In our desperation to succeed in fulfilling the promise we offer God our human solutions, man-made substitutes to the promise. When I first came to Christ, I knew that the Lord wanted me to follow him in some sort of ministry. I was over-enthusiastic and rushed ahead of what he was doing. I left my school where I was training for the arts and expected God to

conform to my time schedule. He didn't and I soon
had to retrace my steps and take up my former position.
Nothing born from fleshly enthusiasm, no matter how
well-intentioned, can substitute for that which comes
from the Spirit.

We must get rid of our Ishmaels before God will
give us Isaac. There is much in the Church today
that is Ishmael, not Isaac. We have stopped short
of the fulfilment and built holy shrines around our
fleshly substitutes. This is particularly obvious in
the charismatic movement, where people are reluctant to let go of the former things, including their
cherished ideas as to how God will work, to make
way for the new move of God's Spirit. Holding
on to the past can reduce what we have to the
status of an Ishmael, who hinders the coming of
Isaac.

The real thing

Yet even here the grace of God shines through.
Provision is made for Ishmael. He is given a promise,
but it is not *the* promise, for he is not the child of
promise. How marvellously God accommodates us
and our weaknesses. But before we use this to excuse
our behaviour, remember that the consequences of
the Ishmael error are with us today. The roots of
bitterness between the Arabs and Israel go back to
that one act of the flesh. It seemed like a good
idea to Abram, a way of fulfilling God's Word.
But it was a costly mistake. In our desire to see
God move and his power released in fulfilment of
his promise, let us be careful never to compromise
with fleshly solutions or to offer man-made substitutes
in place of what God alone can do. And, if we

do slip into the flesh, let us have the courage to admit it and let go of that which is not of the promise; for unless we do that, the promise will never come.

14 Faith Perfected

He did not waver at the promise of God through unbelief, but was strengthened in faith, giving glory to God, and being fully convinced that what He had promised He was also able to perform (Romans 4:20–1).

God's promises are not short-lived. His faithfulness endures long after we would have settled for second-best. Randal had just been made redundant. The American company he had worked for over the past twelve years was closing down its British headquarters and Randal accepted their offer of voluntary redundancy. Married to an English girl called Francis, Randal was able to stay in Britain, but what was he going to do with his life? He and Francis were active youth workers in their local church and the eldership had been praying about asking them to go full-time in the work. Everyone felt that the circumstances were right. God had been speaking to Randal and Francis for a long time, but now they were ready to accept the call. Now it was time for God's best to come forth in their lives.

It was twenty-four years since Abram's first encounter with God. By every indication, Abram was satisfied. He had his son, by his own body. However, it was not Sarai's child and she was not happy. In fact, matters were getting out of hand. She no longer had any place for Hagar, the woman who had usurped her position.

Ishmael had to go: the boy and her mother were driven out. Again we can see the gracious hand of God who had never forgotten the promise, and still had every intention of fulfilling it. Abram was being brought to maturity so that the promise could come forth.

Abram's third encounter with God was entirely different from the rest. The others placed relatively few demands on him – but not this one. Now it was time for Abram to change. The character of the man of God had to come forth, and Abram emerged from this encounter transformed. Every human solution had been tried and had failed. Now at 99 years of age, there was nothing left but the power of God. This time God came in the revelation of another name, and he had another name for Abram too. 'The Lord appeared to Abram and said to him, "I am Almighty God; walk before Me and be blameless"' (Genesis 17:1). The new name of God was *El Shaddai*, which means, 'Almighty God', the God who has power to change us and our circumstances so that they line up with his will. It was a timely reminder to Abram, who by now reckoned his body to be as good as dead, and in the light also of Sarai's barrenness, knew that his situation was beyond all human hope.

This time God calls for a blameless life from Abram. It had been God's will all along, but it was now especially significant because God was emphasising the new level of responsibility required from the one who was to receive the promise of faith. Mature faith must be blameless. It is not that the promise suddenly became conditional upon human obedience, but fulfilment and obedience must go hand in hand. Grace was operating through faith resulting in obedience. Abram fell on his face in submission to El Shaddai, as he heard the promise for the third time in his life, but this time in more detail. It began with the promise of becoming father of many nations:

> As for Me, behold, My covenant is with you, and you shall be a father of many nations. No longer shall your name be called Abram, but your name shall be Abraham; for I have made you a father of many nations. (Genesis 17:4–5)

God then amplified the promise:

> I will make you exceedingly fruitful; and I will make nations of you, and kings shall come from you. And I will establish My covenant between Me and you and your descendants after you in their generations, for an everlasting covenant, to be God to you and your descendants after you. Also I give to you and your descendants after you the land in which you are a stranger, all the land of Canaan, as an everlasting possession; and I will be their God. (Genesis 17:6–8)

Finally, God called for Abraham to embrace the covenant in his own body through the statute of circumcision. This became the covenant sign for all generations. Then God said to Abraham:

> As for you, you shall keep My covenant, you and your descendants after you throughout their generations. This is My covenant which you shall keep, between Me and you and your descendants after you: Every male child among you shall be circumcised; and you shall be circumcised in the flesh of your foreskins, and it shall be a sign of the covenant between Me and you. (Genesis 17:9–11).

At once, Abram saw that his life of faith was not being lived unto himself. Upon *his* obedience depended the flow of God's goodness and revelation to a whole nation and indeed many nations coming after him. His years of waiting and silent suffering fell into place. Maturity is all about accepting responsibility, not just for yourself but for others. Individualism or the enjoyment of mere personal faith, is selfish and immature. The whole revelation from start to finish was about God setting up a relationship between himself and his people, extending to many nations. This relationship was one in which God took total ownership and pride of place over all, summed up in the central promise of the covenant, 'I will be their God, and they will be my people.' It was not just about fulfilling the private ambitions and personal desires of one man.

He was now no longer Abram, 'High or Exalted Father', but Abraham, 'Father of a Multitude', and Sarai too was given a new name, Sarah, meaning 'Princess'. And it was to this couple, one 99 and sterile, the other 90 and barren, that God promised a child: 'Sarah your wife shall bear you a son, and you shall call his name Isaac' (Genesis 17:19), which means laughter.

What's in a name?

These names are significant. *Isaac*, not just because of the joy of lifelong fulfilment, but also because God has the power to make the laughable believable. *Sarah*, because she was being lifted to royal position; and *Abraham* because God had made him the father of many nations. The names spoke of accomplished realities, in the mind of God. They were never anything else. As soon as God speaks it is as good as done.

The Apostle Paul picks up this point in Romans chapter 4, and when referring to the past tense used in Genesis 17:5 says, God 'calls those things which do not exist as though they did' (Romans 4:17). Mature faith has this same confidence and God was encouraging Abraham to say the same thing, and confess his Word. Every time he said his name 'Abraham', his mind would go to the meaning, 'I have made you a father of many nations.' This was faith's confession. He would turn to Sarah and say, 'Princess', kings shall come from you. And he would speak of Isaac not yet born or even conceived, and laugh the laugh of faith, 'Ha! Ha! Ha! Isaac you're on the way!' He did not confess in order to possess; he confessed *because* he possessed. His faith reached maturity. He entered the rest of faith and there was no more struggling and striving to believe.

The New Testament reveals the state of spiritual maturity Abraham attained and in Romans chapter 4 sets out every principle of faith. Abraham's faith began in the promise of God. It was not based on a good idea or even a spiritual notion of Abraham's. It came from God. Anything less would have been presumption. Faith is not what we want, it is what God says. Abraham's faith came by grace, it was not brought by human effort. It was not hyped up by emotionalism or reasoned out by intellectualism. It was God-given: fed and fuelled by the Word, the blood and the Spirit.

Mature faith

Abraham's faith entered into maturity. It was a state where the only thing that mattered was what God had said. And God had said, 'I have made you a father of many nations.' These words were spoken *before* the promise was fulfilled. The assurance of faith is necessary before the promise comes. But Abraham's faith was not any longer in what he could see, touch, taste, smell or hear; his physical senses were of no help. Instead Abraham, 'contrary to hope, in hope believed'. *Against all human expectations and beyond the bounds of all human possibilities, he believed the Word of God.* That is mature faith. He believed, in hope. That is, he believed *before* he saw it fulfilled. Hope belongs to the future, faith holds the promise today. The substance of his faith was at work. He possessed the promise; it was absolutely real to him.

This is how Abraham became a father of many nations, by faith, according to what had been spoken. He faced the facts about his body, which was already dead in respect to fathering a child. He faced the fact that Sarah's womb was dead. But he did not waver. It says that he did not consider these things. He faced them but did not let them dominate his thinking. Instead he reasoned with the mind of faith, 'God has said it. He will do it.' He did not waver through unbelief, but he was strengthened and empowered in his faith. He looked only at the promise. The facts were plain to see – death; but the spiritual truth was stronger than the physical facts, and the God of truth had power to cause every last contrary, physical fact to line up with his will. Abraham was fully convinced that what God had promised he was also able to perform. Abraham knew that God had the power to bring life to his dead body and bring Sarah's womb alive again. Living in praise and keeping the promise fresh in his spirit, he gave glory to God.

We do not know how long Abraham lived in this mature faith, waiting patiently for the time of the promise. It must have been at least a year. But it took him a long time to get there. We must be patient in our ventures of faith. It may take twenty-five years before we see results. Some things come sooner, and other things may take longer. Abraham did not see the total fulfilment in his lifetime, but laid a foundation of faith for future generations. It is that same faith that is working in us, as he is the father of all who believe in Jesus. We can learn from him and it may mean we will have a head start in the journey of faith, especially as we follow Abraham's example of unshakeable confidence in the Word of the promise. The hymn says it well:

Faith, mighty faith the promise sees and looks to that alone,
Laughs at impossibilities and cries, 'It shall be done'!

'Faith without actions is dead', says the Apostle James. And Abraham put his faith into operation. He acted on the Word at the appropriate time and in the appropriate way. And God honoured his Word, before Abraham was a hundred years old: 'And the Lord visited Sarah as He had said, and the Lord did for Sarah as He had spoken. For Sarah conceived and bore Abraham a son in his old age, at the set time of which God had spoken to him' (Genesis 21:1–2).

Faith perfected

But it was not long before Abraham's faith was given a final challenge. God tested Abraham with the command to sacrifice Isaac. He said, 'Take now your son, your only son Isaac, whom you love, and go to the land of Moriah, and offer him there as a burnt offering on one of the mountains of which I shall tell you' (Genesis 22:2). It seems that God was not content with mature faith in Abraham, he wanted to purify it still further. Perfect faith was not in Abraham receiving Isaac, but in sacrificing him on the altar, which he all but did, in obedience to the Lord.

This ultimate test was one of *total* obedience. Would Abraham obey God even in this? It made no sense at all to ask it. It was against God's usual way. In fact human sacrifice would be totally repugnant to him. It was also against the promise of God. Was not Isaac the child of promise, in whom the nations would be blessed? Then why sacrifice him? But Abraham had learned to obey God without question. And, as we shall see, perfect faith was working deep inside him. He knew God and trusted him completely.

The story unfolds, Abraham gets up early and takes his son to the specified place. He says to the servants, 'Stay here with the donkey; the lad and I will go yonder and worship, and we will come back to you' (Genesis 22:5). The first thing we notice, which is also picked up by the writer to the Hebrews, is this remarkable statement of faith, 'We will go and worship God and then we will come back to you.' Abraham seems to have known that if God called him to go through with it all, then he would have to bring the child to life again in order to fulfil the promises made through him! Hebrews says that this is precisely what Abraham believed, and figuratively speaking is exactly what happened (Hebrews 11:19).

The second startling comment is one of the greatest Old Testament statements made about the coming of Christ and his death on the cross. Isaac notices that they have everything with them for worship but no lamb for the sacrifice. To this question Abraham replies, 'My son, God will provide for himself the lamb for a burnt offering.' This is the wisdom of faith, and we do not even need to know whether Abraham fully understood it to see its deep, prophetic character. On Mount Calvary, God did provide the Lamb, the offering of whom opened the way to heaven for all who believe.

The awful moment came: knife in hand, poised ready to plunge it into Isaac's heart. Then suddenly the voice, 'Don't do it, Abraham. Now I know you fear me. You have passed the test.' Abraham's faith was now perfected. He could look on the sacrifice of his son as an act of worship. He could see beyond death to resurrection so that the promise would be fulfilled. By faith Abraham was willing to obey God no matter how ludicrous it seemed and when he could think of a thousand reasons not to. Abraham's faith was perfected beyond the immediate plan of God for himself and, by it, he was able to see truth that would not be commonly known for almost two millennia – God's sacrifice of Christ.

We need to see this kind of commitment to obey God, no matter what the cost today. Jumoke is a vivacious member of our creative ministries team in the church. She was trained in media and the performing arts, and was quite a celebrity at home in Nigeria. Possessing a brilliant jazz voice, she had no shortage of bookings, frequently appearing on television and in theatre productions. Jumoke came to live in Britain, and after some time, felt the Lord ask her to lay down her career.

At first she could not understand it, but then she concluded that as God had given her the talents in the first instance, he had a right to have them back. At that time, she really had no expectation of developing her profession. But since then the Lord has given her back her talent in a totally renewed way. She often sings ministry songs, is involved in British radio and television and helps train other Christians for careers in the needy world of the media and the arts. She has discovered the joy of giving everything back to God.

It is ironic that Isaac, the fulfilment of the promise of faith, might have come between Abraham and God. This shows up real faith for what it is. It is laying hold of God, not things. *Real faith is content with nothing less than God himself.* It lays hold of him as its real object and never lets him go.

15 Faith and Hope

Looking for the blessed hope and glorious appearing of our great God, and Saviour Jesus Christ (Titus 2:13).

At this particular time, God is pouring out his Spirit on the Church in a way that is giving fresh, new hope for the Church of Jesus Christ. For some time many parts of the Christian Church have been losing hope of anything ever happening that would impact our nation. A demoralisation had set in for many churches. Many Christian leaders and ministers have felt dried up, as if there was no real hope of anything ever happening in their ministry and in their church. But with one powerful breath, God is reviving our hope.

One church in London was recently surprised by the Spirit in a particularly dramatic way. It did not have a history of charismatic phenomena, and was if anything opposed to these things. One Sunday, the service went much the same as usual, nothing extraordinary happened at all – that is, until the benediction. The pastor was in the middle of the words, 'May the grace of the Lord Jesus Christ, the love of God, and the fellowship of the Holy Spirit . . . ' and suddenly the Holy Spirit fell on the entire congregation! It looked like a battlefield, with bodies lying everywhere, people laughing in the Spirit and others totally bemused by what was going on. There had been no manipulation or even expectation of these events. It had been totally of God. This event thrust the entire church into a new experience of seeking God. The whole fellowship has a totally new outlook of expectation of what God is wanting to do among them. Hope is being restored.

As you will see in this chapter, hope is bred and fed by faith. It is our faith and our experience of God now by faith that gives us hope and that is a very important balance in the Christian life. The balance is between what we are receiving from God and can receive from God now against what we have to wait for. And it is faith in the present time that gives us perseverance, courage and stickability to hold on to the promise of the return of Jesus Christ and that we shall see him face to face (Titus 2:13; 1 John 3:2–3).

Hope through the Holy Spirit

Now immediately we see how important hope is in the Bible. Romans 15:13 says, 'God is the God of hope' and that he wants us to 'abound in hope'. This is a very important Christian virtue and it can only develop in the power of the Holy Spirit. There is a close connection between faith and hope. As we are filled with all joy and peace in believing, we abound in hope by the power of the Holy Spirit. When the Bible uses the word hope, it doesn't do so in the way we often use it in everyday speech. We may say, 'I hope the bus comes on time', but often it doesn't! Or we say 'I hope that it is going to be sunny on bank holiday Monday.' That's wishful thinking! There is a big difference between this and real, biblical hope. Worldly hope is based on presumption or wishful thinking, and as Christians we have to guard against that.

It is not enough to say, 'I hope I'm saved.' No. You are saved in hope, but it is not enough merely to hope that you are saved. This kind of hope never gets you anywhere. The Bible's revelation on hope is that it is certain knowledge, confident expectation that shall be fulfilled in the future. God wants us to know that we have eternal life, and that we shall see the day of salvation. We are not talking about 'hope so', we are talking about 'know so'. Biblical hope is not vain hope, rooted in presumption or in wishful thinking, rather it is rooted in the revelation of God's Word; God says the future is clear, the future is fixed. God holds the destiny and we are moving towards that destiny, although not in a fatalistic sense, because our destiny is to meet with Jesus face-to-face. Our hope is a living, personal and glorious hope (Titus 2:13).

So we see Bible hope is different from worldly hope. It is something certain. It is something that we can be confident about. It is a present confident expectation, but it *is* to do with the future and the 'not yet'. There are certain things we are going to have to learn to wait for, and waiting is never easy.

Our resurrection body

We are going to have to wait for our resurrection body. We can receive as much healing as God could ever pour into our body, but this body is still going to let us down; it will decay, and one day our spirit is going to separate from our body, in death. As Christians, we should not be fearful of death. We have a hope. We have a confident expectation that if the same Spirit that raised Christ from the dead dwells in us, he shall also give life to our mortal body (Romans 8:11). We need to develop our hope more. I am not negating faith for today, but we need to know how faith applies to tomorrow. Faith has to do with experiencing God today, receiving his promises now, living in his blessing now, but hope fixes our attention on the future blessings of God. Hope is faith directed towards the future.

Faith and hope are twins, closely related to one another and yet different from each other. Like twins, they grow and develop together. The more we grow in faith, the more our hope will grow. The more we believe God now and know of him now, the more confident we will be that we can trust him in the future. I emphasise this because so many people in the Church today argue over these issues. Some people say, for example, 'I'm content, because one day I am going to have it all in heaven.' But there are things that God wants us to have now. Don't wait till you get to heaven! Pie in the sky when you die is all very well, but what's on the plate while we wait? We want a slice now! Don't be superspiritual and say, 'Oh no, no blessing now, only blessings in heaven.' Many of these attitudes are held by us Western Christians because we have been taught to look down on the body and be suspicious of physical blessings.

We are told that healing belongs in heaven; but in heaven we won't need to be healed! The promises of healing are for now! Of course everything will be provided in heaven, but we have a God who also provides now! If we can't trust him with our physical needs, how can we trust him for heaven? Some say, 'I will trust you with my soul, Jesus. But I'll look after my own body!' However, body and soul belong together; and they will be united for ever in the resurrection body. Salvation touches your physical life.

We must not be frightened of the physical life. Some people say, 'Old Testament promises are physical, New Testament promises are spiritual, so don't talk to us about physical promises.' But God has got a whole lot of blessings stored up for us now. He wants us to enter into that part of our inheritance now. There is a down payment now (2 Corinthians 5:5; Ephesians 1:13–14). What a tragedy it would be to get to heaven and ask Jesus, 'Where is my blessing?' and for him to answer, 'Just before we talk about the blessings of my heaven, look at the blessing you missed on the earth, because you were more "spiritual" than me.'

On the other hand, our real orientation is not this earthly life but our future with Christ in heaven. No matter what we experience of him now, it is not worth comparing with what we will have of him then. Despite the many wonderful promises God has given us for this life, the plain fact is that we fall short of so many of them. We miss so much that could be ours and often the reasons are not simple or straightforward. It is not correct, for example, to conclude harshly that when someone fails to be healed, it is because of their sin and unbelief. We do not have hope for this life alone. We are not going to get it all now and that means we do not make this world our home. We have a life to come, where every promise will be ours, including those things that, for whatever reason, we did not find fulfilled on the earth.

Activated by God's Spirit

Our future life in heaven does not mean we have to wait to get there before we get blessed. God says, 'I have blessed you with every spiritual blessing in the heavenly places in Christ Jesus' (Ephesians 1:3). 'Spiritual blessing' here does not mean 'spiritual as opposed to physical'. In this context the word 'spiritual' means 'activated by the Spirit of God'. God has given us many promises. If we can't trust him for our daily life, how can we say we trust him with our eternal destiny? When we prove that God honours his Word here and now, it gives us confidence for the future.

That is why it is important to walk with Jesus closely on the earth, to know him well and to experience every blessing that faith brings into our life, so that our hope can grow. If we learn to experience God now, it strengthens our confidence in him for the future. Hope will definitely affect the way we live now. Hope focuses our attention away from temporal things and fixes our eyes upon eternal things, but it is fed by a faith that gives access to God's blessing now. So hope is essential for practical Christian living. If we are going to invest our life in the right things today, we must have a clear view of the future.

Think of the stock exchange. If you knew what it would be like in twelve months' time, you would know how to invest today. There wouldn't be an investor in the world who wouldn't love to have information like that. If you could see how the market is going to perform in twelve months' time, you would know how to invest now. It would give a whole new meaning to the expression 'futures market'. Well, God has given us that knowledge, not about the market, but about his kingdom. He has shown us the future, he has shown us where to invest our time and our energy, our abilities, our finances, our lives. This world is passing away, and God is going to make a new heaven and a new earth, which is going to be the home of righteousness. We must invest in righteousness now because it is going to flourish in the future kingdom of God. Jesus said, 'Do not lay up for yourselves treasures on earth, where moth and rust destroy and where thieves break in and steal' (Matthew 6:19). All earthly dividends are going to fail. We had better start investing in the future.

Our real future is in heaven

The fundamental orientation of our life must be towards our future in heaven and that is why Jesus says, 'lay up for yourselves treasures in heaven' (Matthew 6:20). Now he is not talking merely of commercial investment, but really about the whole of life. He is saying, 'Invest in the things that matter, that really are important. Put your time into the things that count. Grow the kind of things that are going to bring forth fruit in the future life. Don't just live for this world alone.' Without the confident hope of heaven, life cannot be lived rightly on the earth. Hope gives you a right heavenly mindedness. We need people who live like that. Heaven is your true home. You may not have much of a flat or a rented room, the mortgage may be pretty high, but you have a mansion in heaven! This must become real to us. We have to think biblically, and believe the Word of Jesus. He said, 'In My Father's house are many mansions; if it were not so, I would have told you!' And then he went on to say, 'I am going to prepare a place for you and if I go to prepare a place for you, I will come again and receive you to myself, that where I am you may be also' (John 14:2–3).

I know a family whose son was in the last stages of terminal illness, and through a word of knowledge came to faith in Christ. In the last few days of his life on earth, he opened his heart up to the Lord, totally. One night his father had a dream in which a huge staircase into heaven opened up, and as he walked on the staircase, God said to him, 'This is the house of your son, I have it ready for him.' As he looked inside the house it was magnificent, every favourite thing that his son liked was there in that house. It wasn't long after that, that his son was taken, to live in this house. He went home. This earthly existence is not home! It is a place of pilgrimage only. We are passing through, so don't put too many roots down. I am not saying ignore the earth: it is God's earth, and we must reclaim it for him, but our real future is in the new heaven and the new earth.

A few years ago in Malaysia, I met an old Chinese lady. She was a rough diamond. In fact, she was so rough it was hard to find the diamond! She was in her eighties when she contracted cancer. She had been a Buddhist all her life, but her daughter and son-in-law had come to faith in Christ.

They brought her up from Kuala Lumpur to Penang for some hospital treatment. Just to be with her and to pray the daughter stayed with her night by night. Eventually, the time came when she was not expected to last the night but they kept on praying. Suddenly, the old lady sat up in bed and said, 'I thought all Jesus' disciples were white!' Her daughter said, 'Mama, what are you talking about?' She answered, 'I thought all those disciples were white, but I see twelve Chinese "disciples" of Jesus.' She was seeing Chinese angels! Her daughter said, 'Well, I don't know what you are talking about, mum, but Jesus is for everybody.' Jesus was bringing a revelation to her in the context of her own culture. Prompting her further the daughter asked, 'What are they doing, mum?' The mother replied, 'They are walking around my bed – oh look, they are showing me a house – it is a beautiful house. I am going to go and live there.' The daughter did not understand what was going on. But, in the vision, one of the angels touched the old woman's bed and then left with the rest. She began to recover for a time, and accepted Christ. Then she went home to live in the house the Lord had showed her in the vision. The Lord was saying to her, 'Look, this is your home, but your time has not quite come yet.' She has a mansion in heaven and so have you, if you believe in Jesus. That is your hope, your full inheritance that lies ahead.

The Apostle Peter rejoiced in this truth. He said:

> Blessed be the God and Father of our Lord Jesus Christ, who according to His abundant mercy has begotten us again to a living hope through the resurrection of Jesus Christ from the dead to an inheritance incorruptible and undefiled and that does not fade away, reserved in heaven for you, who are kept by the power of God through faith for salvation ready to be revealed in the last time. (1 Peter 1:3–5)

Vital questions

If our eyes are not fixed on the second coming of Jesus Christ, then we don't know where our hope really lies. Death is not the end. Heaven is our true home, it's where we have our true inheritance, it is where our true hope is coming from. What is your hope today? Do you hope you are going to get married, is that your hope? Is it your career? Is that what you are hoping for? Do you say, 'Oh God, what I want is opportunities to rise in my career'? Noble sentiments maybe, but these are not your hope. *Nothing on the earth can ever be your hope*. Your hope is the blessed hope and the glorious appearing of Jesus Christ our Lord. We have to stir ourselves up with this doctrine and this understanding because we are too comfortable on this earth.

In various places all over the world there is increasing pressure on many churches. Persecution, oppression and even martyrdom is the order of the day.

In these places Christian people are looking to their hope, the coming of Jesus Christ. Unless we can really say, 'Our hope is Jesus', then I don't think we really understand what it is to live the Christian life. It is not just about getting a ticket to heaven, and hoping that it isn't needed too soon! The Bible says we are saved in hope. If we really are saved, not only are we believers, but we are hopers: full of hope, and our hope is the coming of Jesus Christ. We must be ready, he is coming soon.

Jesus is coming!

Finally in this chapter, I want to mention three New Testament Scriptures. First, Titus 2:13: 'Looking for the blessed hope and glorious appearing of our great God and Saviour Jesus Christ.'

The context shows that our hope is on the future coming of Jesus. And this hope has a salutary effect on our behaviour in the present. It encourages us to purify ourselves from ungodliness and to be zealous for good works. It is so important for us to see how our future hope affects our present lives.

Second, 1 John 2:28: 'And now little children, abide in Him, that when He appears, we may have confidence and not be ashamed before Him at His coming.'

Christ is going to come back soon, and we must be ready. Now there are so many views about *how* and *when* he is coming. Whatever our views about the incidentals, one thing is sure – he *is* coming! That is all we really need to know. If you belong to the school of prophecy that believes his coming is not yet, watch out, he could come sooner than you think! And if you belong to the school of thought that says his coming is so close that there is no point in working for change on the earth, watch out, he could wait another thousand years before he returns and hold you responsible for your lack of involvement in society's needs. He is a God of surprises, and he is not going to conform to any of our theories about his coming. *But Jesus is coming!* The knowledge that we are going to see him must affect the way we live now.

Third, 1 John 3:3: 'And everyone who has this hope in Him purifies himself, just as He is pure.'

One of the reasons we have weak Christians today is because we have weak beliefs about tomorrow. The world is not in the hands of political leaders. It is not being controlled by men, or by demons! This world belongs to Jesus. And one day he is going to come and claim it! Yes! We must keep our Christian hope alive. It will teach us how to live today. Hope for the future tells us what to do today.

Hope is the only thing that will see us through. It is not that we have *no* hope for this life. There is a promise in the Bible which corresponds to every need we will ever have for this life. Oh yes, we have hope for this life, but we don't have hope *only* for this life. What we have is a down payment on the future. The more you experience him now the more confident you will be of your future.

16 Faith for the Future

Now may the God of hope fill you with all joy and peace in believing, that you may abound in hope by the power of the Holy Spirit (Romans 15:13).

This is a powerful verse, one of those verses that acts as a spiritual indicator of where we stand in relation to biblical Christianity. Now that is what we want isn't it? We want to have a Bible-based faith. We all want to be biblical Christians; in other words we want to be *real* Christians, and we want to have our lives orientated in the way that God wants them orientated. We want to be facing the right direction with our feet firmly planted on the rock, Christ Jesus. We want to have the right balance in faith and life and living, so that we can be ready to meet the storms and trials of life, and endure into the eternity of God's wonderful future that he has for us. That is what I mean by 'faith for the future'.

Now the spiritual indication in Romans 15:13 is where you stand in this matter of faith and the future. There are three great tests in the Christian life: faith, hope and love, but in this concluding chapter I want to say more about the relationship between faith for today and faith for the future. It is a vitally important issue for the Christian Church today.

Creative tension

The Christian faith is basically orientated towards the future. Do we see Jesus? No. Shall we see Jesus? Yes. Are we saved? Yes, we are saved in as much as we are assured of our destiny, but we are not yet saved in the sense that we have arrived at our destination. We are on a journey: a journey towards a destination that lies in the future. And if we are not facing the direction of the future and moving towards that, then we are not on the journey at all.

As we have seen, to be a Christian means not just to have faith: it also means to have hope. The hope of the Gospel is the salvation of your entire spirit, soul and body (1 Thessalonians 5:23). It is a future event. Yet many of us don't understand this creative tension between faith for today and the future God promises us. There is a creative tension between the 'now' and the 'not yet', between what we enjoy now and what we have to wait for patiently. It seems that the things God wants us to have now we are reluctant to receive and the things that God says wait for we must have now. God says, 'Get this tension right', and this verse helps us. First of all he says, 'I am the God of hope, the God of tomorrow!' The God of faith is the God of today and the God of tomorrow.

This understanding is sadly missing from much of modern Christianity. In the early days of this century, when our church, Kensington Temple, was founded, Elim preachers declared a fourfold message, a four-fold Gospel. They preached Jesus Christ as *Saviour*, the one who forgives sins. They proclaimed him as *Healer*, the one through whom we can now enjoy physical blessing and physical provision. They lived with the expectation of a touch of God upon their lives, and knew God was concerned about the sickness in their body or the amount of food that was in the cupboard at home. They also announced him as the *Baptiser in the Holy Spirit*, the one who brings the very presence of heaven in our souls, the Holy Spirit, the divine foretaste of the future life. The final part of this great message spoke about faith for the future. They heralded Christ as the *Coming King*, the one coming to bring God's ultimate future into the present.

It was a popular message sweeping many thousands into the kingdom of God. Men like the Jeffries brothers, George and Stephen, together with many other Pentecostal pioneers are the undervalued heroes of twentieth-century British Christianity. They preached an uncompromising Gospel of supernatural faith. Their message was perhaps the most balanced and biblical of all the evangelists, holding the correct tension between the 'now' and the 'not yet'. They had the 'now' of forgiveness, healing and physical provision, and the 'now' of fullness in the Holy Spirit. But they also balanced all of that against the constant reminder and challenge of the second coming of Christ, the 'not yet' of future hope.

This is the creative tension God intends. The more we experience faith in the present, the more our faith for the future is strengthened. God is a God of hope and he wants to 'fill us with joy and peace in believing' (Romans 15:13). Whatever our circumstances, faith will give us joy. Whatever our circumstances, faith will give us peace. We have joy and peace in believing. But then Paul goes on to say 'that you may abound in hope.' So the more faith we have, the more hope we have. The more of him we know today, the more we can trust him for tomorrow. Our world needs hope. People are failing because they do not have confidence for the future, but Christians can stand like a lighthouse in the midst of a stormy ocean, a beacon of light shining hope into the world. With Jesus there is hope for our lives. There is hope for marriages, there is hope for our children, because we serve a God of hope. The more we strengthen our faith and grow in faith, the more we will abound in hope by the Holy Spirit.

The 'now' and the 'not yet'

We must have a creative tension between the 'now' of faith and the 'not yet' of hope. The great Apostle John certainly knew this. He writes, 'Beloved, now we are children of God; and it has not yet been revealed what we shall be, but we know that when He is revealed, we shall be like Him, for we shall see Him as He is' (1 John 3:2). Three times it says 'shall be', speaking of our future. John says, 'Now we are the children of God, but what we shall be has not yet been revealed.' There is a 'now' and a 'not yet'. And the way we relate these two together creatively is the key to successful Christian living.

There are so many benefits that we can experience now. Just think of some of the benefits God gives to his children now. Peace with God (Romans 5:1), provision for our physical needs (Matthew 6:31–3), and eternal life (1 John 5:11–13). And in addition to these, we have joy, access into God's grace, deliverance, protection and his presence. All that is *our present experience*. Let's enjoy it!

There is one prayer that we will never stop praying on earth and God will never stop answering and that is, *'More* Lord!' When I was a little child, I was always asking for second helpings. My mother used to make the most delicious apple pie: you could smell it five miles away! After the meal, she would take the biggest slice of pie and put it on my plate and it would come down with a thud, and I would grab the nearest implement next to me and I began to ask, 'Is there any more?' 'Eat what's on your plate first!' was her usual rejoinder.

So many people ask, 'Lord, how much is available?' and they start getting all technical about it: 'How much is on the plate? What proportion is that to the rest of the pie?' Now I don't know (and I don't think anyone knows) how big that slice is. I don't know how much is available now. But I do know one thing, he wants us to eat what is on the plate! And I am certain of this too, that we will never in this life come to an end of experiencing the delight of that which is upon the plate. Never. He will always say, 'Take, eat and enjoy. Ask, I *will* give, I *will* bless, I *will* strengthen, I *will* provide.' God is a God of blessing and that blessing is for the here and now.

But at the same time the Bible says, 'What we shall be has not yet been revealed', which means we have not even begun to experience what we shall have one day. The whole orientation of God's book is towards the future. What we see and have now is not all there is! There is a future beyond this world, which is where our real orientation is. Our real desire is not for anything that can be experienced in this life. Think about all those people that Jesus healed. They were healed completely and permanently, but they still died in the end. When Jesus healed them, he didn't transform them to a resurrected body. Even when Lazarus was raised from the dead, he was brought back to his former mode of physical life. But our hope goes beyond that.

Glorious freedom

The Bible says that the same Spirit which raised Christ

from the dead dwells in us and he will give life to our mortal bodies (Romans 8:11). For we were saved in this hope: the hope that our own bodies which are subject to the bondage of decay, should be transformed in the resurrection. We shall have a spiritual body, a new body capable of enjoying everything that God has for us. Our bodies let us down. When God shows himself even in an infinitesimal amount of his power, most of us collapse and spend the rest of the time on the floor! That's why people fall down under the power of God. This mortal body is capable of holding the blessings of the kingdom, only to a point. In other words, we need a new body: a body that can take the blessing of God. The blessing of God is so strong, so powerful that we, in our present mode of existence, are physically incapable of holding it.

So the Bible says that our hope as Christians is resurrection, not resuscitation, or being brought back to this life. Neither is this mere immortality of the soul, but it is being given a brand new life from God and a new body that goes with it, a body like his glorious body (1 Corinthians 15:42–9). When we see him, we shall be like him and we shall see him as he is (1 John 3:2). That is our *blessed* hope.

And so as we believe him now for the present blessings we are building an unshakeable faith for the future. That is why he has given us so many blessings now, so that we can be confident in the blessings of the future. After all, we are all going to face that final test of standing before God. What will your confidence be then? You won't be able to say, 'Oh Lord, I put in a good attendance at my church.' That won't cut any ice with God. The only thing that will give you confidence, at that time, is our knowledge of him now. So the more you trust him for healing and for finances, the more you enter into his promises now, the stronger our faith will be to face that future.

So as the God of hope fills us with all joy and peace in believing, he causes our hope to abound. We know where we stand in relation to this by how much we think about the return of Jesus, by how much we long to see Jesus. That is how much we are living for him now. I pointed out earlier that this was an indicator text, a test of our current spiritual state. This understanding leads us towards the right balance in the question of spiritual fulfilment. But unless we balance faith for now and faith for the future we may fall prey to two dangers.

Triumphalism (over-realised eschatology)

The doctrine of the end times is called eschatology: what happens at the end. Triumphalism is over-realised eschatology and is the error of saying that you can have 'everything now', and do not have to wait until heaven. It is the doctrine of the spiritually greedy. This is the attitude which says, 'I do not want to wait, I want my inheritance now.' It ignores the future element in salvation and leads to spiritual immaturity and selfish demands. There were some people in the city of Corinth whom Paul called 'super apostles' and this is how he describes them in 1 Corinthians 4:8–9: 'Already you are full, you have already filled yourselves with God's blessings.' He says, 'You are already rich – talk about prosperity, you are full of it! You are reigning as kings. For *you*, the kingdom has come!' But then he adds, 'And you have done all of that without us.' He says, 'I indeed could wish that you were kings and did reign, so that we could come and reign with you.' I would paraphrase Paul's next words like this, 'But I will tell you how it really is with us apostles. It seems from our lifestyle that God has taken us and displayed us last, as men condemned to death. For we have been made a spectacle to the world. Both to angels and to men.' What's he talking about? He is saying we belong at the end of the queue, at the end of the line. The end of the victory parade was where you found the defeated ones, the prisoners of war, while those who had conquered were at the front. Paul says, 'If you want to look at me you won't find me boasting at the front. You will find me at the back with the prisoners.'

This is the Apostle Paul speaking; how can he use such a negative image? Because that was the reality for him. Living the life of faith was not lapping up the 'good life', but one of true service and sacrifice. He was beaten, flogged, shipwrecked and on occasions left for dead. He sometimes went without food, clothing and sleep. All this was in the name of faith. It was not that he could not believe God for miraculous provision; he knew more about that than anyone. He had confident faith in the God of abundance. But he lived for the future, for eternal things and made his choices accordingly.

Those people in Corinth wanted to be up at the front where there was plenty of glory but no sacrifice. They wanted to wear the crown without carrying the cross. But God's offer is first the cross, then the crown. First the suffering and the identification with the Christ of the cross, then you will know victory. *There is no short cut to glory.* Unless you have faith for the future, you won't put up with present suffering with Christ for one moment, you will rather go and join the pleasure seekers. Jesus said, 'Take up the cross daily', and until we have confidence in the future we will never do it. We will only want blessings now, to be happy now.

But sometimes we have to live with large areas of unfulfilment.

I am not saying we can't live a victorious life on the earth. What Paul really means is that the way to conquer is to carry your cross. The way to get a crown is to carry that cross. Jesus stooped to conquer. But there are many people who are more committed to comfortable living than they are willing to identify with the poor, the sick and the needy. They want to live in the lap of luxury, while the sick and the needy are not in luxurious surroundings. The rich are needy, and they need ministry too, but there are some people who are so taken up with a wrong idea of faith that they would never sacrifice to reach anyone for Jesus. The Apostle Paul's attitude was totally different. He refused the comfortable option of a secure ministry in Antioch, and went where God told him to go, whether there was a love offering or not, whether the accommodation was a palace, a humble home or a prison!

Until we know that our real future is not in this life, there will be no sacrificial service in the Church of Jesus Christ. One quarter of the world's population today doesn't know anything about Jesus because we are reluctant to suffer for the Gospel. A quarter of the world today is culturally and geographically excluded from the Gospel because we are refusing to pay the price of a cross-carrying Christianity. A real life of faith will do something about that. But there is also another extreme to avoid.

Defeatism (under-realised eschatology)

The proper balance does not sit at the other extreme of living a defeatist form of Christianity. We may call this an under-realised eschatology, and it too is seriously contrary to New Testament teaching. For many, the promises of God that have anything to do with physical blessings belong in the future, and they say, 'You can't expect it now. You'll get it in heaven but you won't get it on the earth.' In contrast, the Bible teaches that the kingdom has begun. *The fullness is yet to be, but there are blessings now*. Some people are carrying their cross so much that they are just plain miserable. They have forgotten that on the other side of the crucifixion lies resurrection. Many are saying, wait until we get to heaven, but we need to see some triumphs now. We have got to know what it is to be victorious in this life and in this experience. But it is not the victory of those people who take a short cut to the throne. I want to wait until Jesus says, 'Come on, now is the time.' In the meantime, if it takes suffering – yes! If it takes sacrifice – yes! If it takes self-denial – yes! That is real faith.

Biblical realism

The real solution to the tension between the today of faith and the tomorrow of hope is what I call biblical realism. To the triumphalist, suffering is a vice; to the defeatist, suffering is a virtue, but to the balanced Christian, it is a reality to be faced by faith and hope. Faith deals with what can be changed and hope deals with the rest by patiently waiting for the deliverance to come. There is a fullness yet to be, and we have hardly even begun to imagine it! But there is also a foretaste now! God the Holy Spirit has revealed it to us. The Holy Spirit, who is the down payment, the deposit of our inheritance and life with Christ, gives us a delightful indication of what is to come (Ephesians 1:12–13), and this is how God deals with our practical needs now. He knows we have such needs and has made full provision for them.

But in the midst of it all, we do not have such a claim on God that we are exempt from all suffering, all pain and misery. We are subject to these things as frail flesh and as part of the fallen physical world. We therefore believe God for today and trust him for all our needs in this life, but the fundamental orientation of our lives is toward the future blessing, and we are prepared, if necessary, to endure now so that we can enjoy later everything in his kingdom. As Paul says, 'For I consider that the sufferings of this present time are not worthy to be compared with the glory which shall be revealed in us' (Romans 8:18).

Think too of the following Scriptures, all of which stress the same point:

For now we see in a mirror, dimly, but then face to face. Now I know in part, but then I shall know just as I also am known (1 Corinthians 13:12).

Beloved, now we are children of God; and it has not yet been revealed what we shall be, but we know that when He is revealed, we shall be like Him, for we shall see Him as He is (1 John 3:2).

For we know that if our earthly house, this tent, is destroyed, we have a building from God, a house not made with our hands, eternal in the heavens. For in this we groan, earnestly desiring to be clothed with our habitation which is from heaven (2 Corinthians 5:1–2).

The Spirit Himself bears witness with our spirit that we are children of God, and if children, then heirs of

God and joint heirs with Christ, if indeed we suffer with Him, that we may also be glorified together. For I consider that the sufferings of this present time are not worthy to be compared with the glory which shall be revealed in us. For the earnest expectation of the creation eagerly waits for the revealing of the sons of God (Romans 8:16–19).

And I heard a loud voice from heaven saying, 'Behold, the tabernacle of God is with men, and He will dwell with them, and they shall be his people. God Himself will be with them and be their God. And God will wipe away every tear from their eyes; there shall be no more death, nor sorrow, nor crying. There shall be no more pain, for the former things have passed away (Revelation 21:3–4).

The balance of faith

These verses do not present that brand of super-spirituality which calls *suffering a vice*. They do not teach that Christians can have everything now. Nor do they claim that *suffering is a virtue*, and that God is not interested in the needs of this life. Over-realised eschatology is unrealistic, unattainable and totally selfish. It has no room for the theology of suffering or for the challenge of mission. Ultimately it is the gospel of Hedonism, or selfish pleasure with no sacrifice and no cross.

However, under-realised eschatology is also wrong. It appeals to the religious spirit. This equally unbalanced brand of super-spirituality claims that God is not interested in the needs of this life. It's only agony *now*, ecstasy *later*, only misery *now*, joy *later*, suffering *now*, glory *later*. This harsh religious view says that to be poor or sick is to be spiritual and teaches that God is not really concerned about physical blessings. Both these views are unhelpful. Biblical realism, on the other hand, says that Christians are meant to live out and experience *to the full* everything that God has for us now. It is to live life trusting God, believing him for *every* promise. It is to accept that many of God's promises extend to the physical realm. It is also to understand that there is no such thing as 'everything now' and that there is no short cut to the kingdom. Spiritual maturity appreciates that whatever we can and do experience of God now is but a pale reflection of what we shall know and enjoy.

Hope gives perseverance

Faith for tomorrow gives perseverance for today. This is surely what Paul means in Romans 8:25: 'But if we hope for what we do not see, we eagerly wait for it with perseverance.' Hope by its very nature remains unseen and in the future. That is why our hope strengthens us to keep on going until we arrive at the destination. It is this balance between faith – what we enjoy now – and hope – what we are waiting for – that enables us to endure all things until the end comes. When that end finally comes it will be the glorious destiny of all things. Hope never disappoints. In another part of Romans, Paul says, 'Therefore having been justified by faith, we have peace with God through our Lord Jesus Christ, through whom also we have access by faith into this grace in which we stand and rejoice in hope of the glory of God. And not only that, but we also glory in tribulation' (Romans 5:1–3). True biblical hope will give Christians perseverance in trials, and this is why we glory in tribulation, 'knowing that tribulation produces perseverance; and perseverance, character'.

God knows how to get character into us and if we have no faith for the future, we will misunderstand his actions now. God is working something in you, because he wants you to be strong. Get rid of childish demands – the me, me, me type of Christianity. God will allow you to have troubles, but you can glory in them because they work character, and what does character produce? Hope, faith for the future. In other words, the stronger you are as a Christian, the stronger your hope is. Your faith today feeds your confidence for the future. The stronger your faith, the more firmly fixed your eyes will be upon him and you will know this as you will know nothing else, Jesus never fails. *He never fails.*

They loved not their lives

Whatever he calls us to go through in our life of faith, our trials and our tribulations, the more we experience of him now, the more healing we receive, the more we stand strong, the more we stand on our relationship with him, the stronger our character. And we will be able to hold out for the future. In these end times, God is looking for a people who will know the meaning of the Word: 'They overcame him by the blood of the Lamb and the word of their testimony' (Revelation 12:11). They overcome, 'because they loved not their lives to the death'. That is what the whole Spirit-filled community has to learn. We must stop loving our life and learn to lose it. If our hope truly is in heaven, then we will live now like a real Christian.

I call to mind the young man who has gone to glory to wear a martyr's crown, martyred one mile from Kensington Temple. Not in an Islamic nation, or in communist China, but Alfredo was martyred for Christ one mile from our church building. He loved not his life unto the death. One night he got out of a car to stop a young man from being murdered in a drug-related street fight. He was soon caught up in the situation, and was fatally stabbed. When that knife plunged into him it severed five major organs. I went to hospital to raise him from the dead if necessary, with, I felt, no shortage of faith. But he wasn't only living by faith, he was also living in this hope. He recovered consciousness only long enough to pray, 'Lord Jesus, take me home.' He was living in the hope of what would be his in the resurrection and the future kingdom of God.

We need a generation of Christians who know how to have faith for the future as well as belief for today, because our hope is not for this life only. Our hope is for that which is to come and we live now in the light of that. We will overcome by the blood of the Lamb. We will overcome by the word of our testimony and by not loving our life unto the death. That is the contract, those are the terms, those are the conditions. Now we will not all have the privilege of laying our lives down physically. He chooses some to wear the martyr's crown for eternity, but all of us have the privilege of laying our lives down continually. We do so practically on the altar of consecration, on the altar of service, on the altar of dedication, on the altar of Christian commitment, and we will never do it until we know what it is to hope as well as to believe.

I was married in June 1979, and on our wedding day I gave Amanda a card, which has been framed and hangs in our kitchen. It reads, 'The future is as bright as the promises of God.' It was reassuring to know this as we began our future together. Since that time we have had many trials, disappointments, personal losses and failures of all kinds. But through it all, we have always known God's faithfulness, his joy and strength and his patience as we have struggled to learn the lessons he was teaching us.

Despite the difficulties of life from which none of us is immune, we can know a real confidence and peace within as we face the future. The natural uncertainties of life do not rob us of the spiritual certainties of faith. Rather faith gives us a confidence to face the future and our hope assures us that the future is bright. An Old Testament verse confirms this: 'For I know the thoughts that I think toward you says the Lord, thoughts of peace and not of evil, to give you a future and a hope' (Jeremiah 29:11). Or, in the words of the hymn writer:

> Faith for today and bright hope for tomorrow,
> Blessings all mine, with ten thousand beside.
> Great is Thy faithfulness!

Because of God's faithfulness today and his promises for tomorrow, we can have a faith that will never fail.